THE
OLD
MONEY
BOOK

Other books by Byron Tully:

Old Money Style: The Gentleman's Edition

— • —

Old Money, New Women: How To Manage
Your Money & Your Life

— • —

The Hindu Way To Wealth – My Private
Coversations with One of India's Richest Men

— • —

The Old Money Money Guide To Marriage:
Getting Right – Making It Last

THE
OLD
MONEY
BOOK

HOW TO LIVE BETTER WHILE SPENDING LESS

2nd Edition
Expanded & Updated

Secrets of America's Upper Class

BYRON TULLY

The Old Money Book
2nd EDITION

First edition printed in 2013

Edited by Weatherford Bradley
Cover photo by Weatherford Bradley | Copyright 2020 | All rights reserved.
Cover and book design by Kedi Darby

ISBN: 978-1-950118-12-0 (Paperback)
ISBN: 978-1-950118-13-7 (Hardback)

CONTENTS

——— ◆ ———

Forward..vii

Introduction xiii

– *Part I* –

CORE VALUES

HEALTH..23
That Was Then. This Is Now. 31

EDUCATION...50
That Was Then. This Is Now. 60

THE WORK ETHIC 64
That Was Then. This Is Now. 71

ETIQUETTE & MANNERS.................................77
That Was Then. This Is Now. 86

FINANCIAL INDEPENDENCE....................92
That Was Then. This Is Now. 104

FAMILY & MARRIAGE 118
That Was Then. This Is Now. 126

CONTENTS

PRIVACY 136

That Was Then. This Is Now. 141

– Part II –

HOW OLD MONEY DOES IT

ATTIRE 151

That Was Then. This Is Now. 167

DICTION & GRAMMAR 193

That Was Then. This Is Now. 196

FURNISHINGS 198

That Was Then. This Is Now. 205

READING 207

That Was Then. This Is Now. 210

HOUSING 213

That Was Then. This Is Now. 216

SOCIALIZING 221

That Was Then. This Is Now. 226

CARS 233

That Was Then. This Is Now. 241

TRAVEL 243

That Was Then. This Is Now. 251

STAFF vs. SERVICES 265

That Was Then. This Is Now. 267

SUMMARY 268

FORWARD

———— ◆ ————

When I wrote *The Old Money Book* in 2013, the global economy was still crawling its way back from the Financial Crisis of 2008. During that time, I had watched friends, colleagues, and most of America suffer in ways not seen since the Great Depression. Housing prices had plummeted. Unemployment had spiked. Foreclosures were common. People were selling their jewelry. College students returned home, their parents unable to continue to pay for their tuition. Many young adults, once gainfully employed with big plans for the future, moved back in with Mom and Dad to regroup, rethink, and look for any kind of work.

America's eternal optimism had taken a serious hit, but the United States government took action. Banks—if not working people—were bailed out of the situation quickly. Mortgage assistance was put in place. Investment and entrepreneurship rallied. And slowly, many went back to work, back to "normal," and tried to forget the whole thing.

Not me. I saw the moment as a wake-up call.

Living in Los Angeles among an apparently affluent demographic, I witnessed how precariously many seemingly "rich" people lived: if they lost their jobs, they were about three months away from financial disaster. Why? Because they were spending everything they earned...and then some. They lived in the McMansion. They drove the luxury car. They sported the latest designer fashions and logo-heavy accessories.

Still, the math goddess that reigns over income and expenses was unimpressed, and many had to downsize considerably. A few lost everything.

These horror stories stood in stark contrast to my friends in Boston, some who came from old, established New England families. While they shared the same worries about the economy and the country during the crisis, their financial position remained sound. Their modest, much-below-their-means and far-under-the-radar manner of living changed not one bit. Their concerns were for others, not for themselves. Why? Because they had been raised with or had adopted a way of life that was antithetical to the "consumer'" lifestyle that so many Americans had been sold.

They lived in older but well-cared-for houses. They drove nondescript cars. They dressed modestly and traditionally in what some might call "preppy" attire. Most importantly, they prioritized savings and investment above conspicuous consumption. They were more concerned with actually *being financially independent* rather than *looking rich*.

In making this distinction, they embraced different values. They shifted their priorities. These priorities led them to make different choices. These choices led them to develop different habits, and experience different, decidedly better, outcomes in their financial and personal lives. Especially when the chickens came home to roost, as they did in 2008.

As I said, some of these people were raised in this culture of Old Money, and some simply adopted its practices. Both groups benefited equally. All weathered the downturn relatively unscathed.

Watching this phenomenon in real time, I realized that there were important lessons here for people who wanted to live better while spending less. It simply came down to making the distinction between aspiring to a certain *standard of living* and curating a certain *quality of life*.

I took this concept in hand and wrote *The Old Money Book*, detailing the values, priorities, and habits of America's upper class in order to show anyone from any background how to live a richer life. It's that simple. There's no snobbery to it (quite the opposite, in fact). It's not a "get rich quick" scheme (again, quite the opposite). There's no social media group to join, no webinar to sign up for, no logo, no slogan, no merchandise, and, tragically, no secret society with oaths sworn in Latin or initiation rituals that include blindfolds and torches.

After *The Old Money Book*, several related volumes followed, including:

- *The Old Money Guide To Marriage*, which offers insights into dating and relationships;

- *Old Money, New Woman: How To Manage Your Money and Your Life*, which details the challenges and opportunities facing women today; and

- *Old Money Style: The Gentleman's Edition*, which provides a timeless approach to dressing well for men.

Even though I was still curating *The Old Money Book* blog in the fall of 2019, I felt fairly confident that my work on this subject was done.

Then came the COVID-19 pandemic. And as the famous saying goes, it was *déjà vu* all over again. This time the culprit was not overhyped mortgage-backed securities but a deadly, airborne virus that decimated the global economy. Worse than that, as I write this, it has infected millions of people and taken almost one million lives.

Originating in China, the virus quickly spread throughout that country, into Europe, and then hit the northeast of the United States like a tsunami. Devastating statistics rose from New York City. Other metropolitan areas in the country soon experienced "clusters" of infections. Healthcare services were, and still remain, strained to the limit, mirroring the nerves of many Americans. Stimulus payments and recovery packages have been legislated, and will, most likely, continue in an effort to calm financial markets and moderate the suffering of millions of people who were living paycheck to paycheck before this disaster.

Unprecedented quarantines of entire cities and the shutdown of daily life (and commerce) became routine and widespread—and may continue. The "lull" that scientists and political leaders predicted would occur during the spring and summer months of 2020 never materialized. In fact, the spread accelerated. And while businesses and schools have reopened, or tried to, the global economy has been left hollowed out. Again, unemployment figures continue their gasp-inducing climb. Mass foreclosures for homeowners and mass evictions for families who rent appear imminent, like black clouds on the horizon.

As the entire world waits for a vaccine or treatment to be discovered or developed, and then distributed to the global population, nobody's talking about "getting back to normal." We seem to all be trying to decipher or determine what the "new normal" is going to look like. We're trying to find that opportunity that wise men say lies in the ruins of every disaster, that flower blooming among the weeds, that dawn on the horizon.

And, once again, I have watched this slow-motion train wreck unfold, not from Los Angeles, but this time from Paris. Once again I witness a seismic shock of a sudden economic downturn and the aftershocks of financial and personal suffering that follow. Many people I know have weathered this storm better than that of 2008. After the financial crisis, they changed their priorities. They downsized. They started—and stayed with—a savings and debt reduction plan. They went back to work or got a second job, and turned a corner in how they lived their lives. Even if it was uncomfortable, they learned from that pain and adapted when they had the chance.

However, not everyone who went through the financial crisis changed their spending habits. Many continue to spend plenty, waste much, and save little. Some people have circumstances so dire that they have nothing to save at the end of each month, even if they wanted to. Either way, millions of people are struggling every day to get a handle on their personal situation during economic crisis and health crisis, and simply survive it.

I can't help much with the health crisis. I can, however, reintroduce you to the Core Values of Old Money and offer you the time-tested insights on How Old Money Does It. These concepts and strategies have not changed. They will always serve you well.

What *has* changed is the context in which the opportunity now exists. For many, it is now urgent to make changes in lifestyle and spending. Some of the amended recommendations I make in this version of *The Old Money Book* reflect that urgency. Some measures suggested here are geared toward immediate survival, not just general ideas on how someone might, at their leisure, consider, you know, maybe one day reprioritizing their life if it seems like something they might want to do. This second edition of *The Old Money Book* is more a manual on how to respond to a house on fire than how to respond to a dinner invitation.

Other additions to this book reflect changes in my personal perspectives over the past seven years. Like most people, I've had experiences that have altered my opinions and perspectives on certain subjects. I have not deleted any of the material I presented in the original version of *The Old Money Book*. I have added a "That Was Then, This Is Now" segment in places I feel it important to elaborate upon, modify, or correct ideas that I presented pre-COVID-19. I have also added posts from *The Old Money Book* blog that might offer insight and inspiration during this difficult time.

Obviously, the world has changed drastically and dramatically. Because of this, what we consider to be "good information" must necessarily, to some degree, be "current information" if it is to retain its value. What we refer to as "wisdom," of course, is something that remains true regardless of the changing times.

In this second edition of the book, I have attempted to strike this balance between that timely information and enduring wisdom. Given the current dynamics of the pandemic, political unrest, and economic uncertainty in which I offer these revisions and additions, the endeavor may be likened to performing brain surgery in a rowboat, at night, in a storm.

Still, it is work that I feel must be done.

As always, I hope that you and your family remain safe and healthy in this bizarre and often distressing world. As you digest the information in this book and consider how to apply it in your life, I hope you'll remember the words of Emily Dickinson, who wrote, "Not knowing when the dawn will come, I open every door."

Stay optimistic. Open every door. We will prevail.

Byron Tully
September 2020
Paris, France

INTRODUCTION

The Purpose of this Book

The purpose of this book is to help people who want to live fuller, happier, and more productive lives do so by learning about and emulating the values, priorities, and habits of "Old Money." The term "Old Money" refers to individuals whose families have enjoyed wealth and privilege for three generations or more.

In the United States, "Old Money" generally refers, but is not limited, to established families in the northeast of the country whose ancestors accumulated large amounts of money and then invested and spent it in a certain way. In Europe, Asia, Africa, and the Middle East, "Old Money" may include aristocratic and royal families as well, most of whom are not household names.

These families have lived in a certain way and raised their children in a certain way, which tended to ensure the preservation of their wealth and the happiness and overall well-being of their descendants. Many of these descendants are still benefiting from this way of life, both financially and emotionally. Therefore, anyone wishing to experience financial independence, wealth, and happiness in their own lives might do well to study this way of life and adopt its principles.

Please note: the possession of money alone for a period of time does not mean that a family or a person is Old Money. To be Old Money definitely requires money, but also refers to a set of values and a way of life that are detailed in this book.

Ironically, enjoying and benefiting from the values and way of life of Old Money does not require money, but will often result in the accumulation of it.

What This Book Is and Is Not

This book is a guide. It is by no means the final word on the subject, but the fundamental concepts in it are accurate, enduring, and sound. To be beneficial, the information in it must be assimilated by each individual reader and applied appropriately to his or her life. This is best done gradually and thoughtfully. One small habit is worth a thousand drastic changes.

This book was written because so many in the middle class, especially in America, have had good incomes, but after years of hard work, have little or nothing to show for it. This book may show anyone of any income level or social class how to keep more of the money earned or inherited while increasing the overall enjoyment of life. Given the current state of the global economy, this book may also help anyone do more with less.

The suggestions in this book on such topics as wardrobe and furnishings can easily be followed; one can simply go buy new clothes and furniture in an attempt to act like Old Money. Whoopee damn doo. The way Old Money dresses and lives is symptomatic of its values, not the core of them; these values may require more time, effort, and discipline to understand, adopt, and put into practice. However, they tend to pay handsome dividends in quality of life.

This book is not a guide on how to get rich. Most people become wealthy through vision, hard work, calculated risk, and no small amount of luck. They stay rich by adhering to the principles detailed herein. If you are newly rich, this book may help you preserve your wealth...and your sanity. If your family is already rich, this book will detail many of the concepts you've experienced but may not have been able to articulate.

This book is not about how to marry rich. Most people who marry for money earn every penny of it and seldom find permanent wealth or happiness. But if you genuinely seek to marry well, this book may offer insight into what contributes to an enduring, fulfilling relationship.

This book is not about passing yourself off as rich. Acting like a snob is the very antithesis of Old Money, so pass yourself off somewhere else.

This book is brief and to the point. Old Money and the author abhor waste.

An Overview

A cornerstone of Old Money thinking is to prioritize personal reality over public perception. This means that Old Money is more concerned with the way things actually are with their personal situation than the way they appear to others.

In short, Old Money doesn't much care what other people think, as confirmed by the colorful pants some Old Money men wear and the nicknames some of the Old Money women go by (wink, nod).

Personal reality is the amount of money one actually has; public perception is the amount of money one wants others to *believe* one has.

Old Money has a strong identity that is rooted in self, work, and family, not in material possessions and not in perceptions of social status, and certainly not in fame. Material possessions can be lost or stolen, and social status is an illusion. One's contributions to family in particular and society in general through hard work, discipline, discretion, and charity are much more important than public opinion or approval.

A life built on purpose, infused with poise, filled with joy, and framed with self-imposed guidelines for what is and is not permissible, is preferable. Being inner-directed and seeking approval from oneself rather than others leads to greater fulfillment. Judging others is not necessary. Proclaiming one's accomplishments is in poor form. Old Money speaks softly, and says so much in doing so.

Old Money does not do what is illegal, and may not do even what is legal if it is not ethical. Old Money holds itself to a higher standard: its own. If talent does what it can and genius does what it must, Old Money does what it should.

Old Money does what is best for the long term, not what might only be pleasant or immediately expedient.

The Philosophy

The philosophy of Old Money is to enjoy life to the fullest; to learn and grow as a person; to work hard and excel in a profession that one enjoys and is passionate about; to preserve and expand one's financial resources while using them well; to share a rich life with friends and family; to explore the world in order to better understand it, and one's place in it; to prepare one's children for a productive, healthy, and rewarding life of their own; to benefit society and its less fortunate members through charitable giving or vocation; to leave a legacy for future generations.

The Basics

The basics of Old Money are its values. These are the concepts it holds dear which evolve into priorities. These priorities dictate the order and manner in which choices are made with the resources available. The resources available are most obviously time and money, but also include opportunity. The choices you make with time, money, and opportunity shape your future and determine, to a large extent, the quality of your life.

An Example

One example is worth a thousand proclamations. So let's consider a hypothetical but all too common scenario to illustrate the philosophy, values, priorities, and resulting actions of Old Money, in contrast with...someone else.

Someone else is Jim. Jim, who is not Old Money, is a young, single working guy with a college degree and few commitments, living in an apartment. He is saving some money, but generally living paycheck to paycheck. When Uncle Harry dies, he leaves Jim one million dollars in his will. Jim is ecstatic. He deposits the check for one million dollars, quits his job immediately and tells all his friends and family the good news. He throws a party. Women suddenly find him incredibly intelligent and attractive (wink, nod). He buys an expensive car—which he pays cash for—and an expensive watch and some fine new clothes, paying retail prices for everything.

But it's not just about him. He's a good son, so he buys his mother a new house and the new car she'd always dreamed about, and he sends her on a cruise, too. "Financial advisors" come from every direction. They stroke Jim's ego, explaining that his new position requires shrewd investment advice, generally involving hot stock tips, timeshares, and other can't-miss opportunities. Friends suddenly have emergencies or pressing needs and come to Jim for loans, which they will surely repay in the very near future. These same friends now hang out with Jim nights and weekends, suggesting dinner and drinks, clubs and restaurants, all of which Jim ends up paying for. Some other friends have grown resentful of Jim's good fortune and the way he handled it, and have drifted away.

A few months later, maybe even a year later, the shine has worn off the inheritance and the hangover sets in. The luxury car needs expensive maintenance. The property taxes are due on Mom's new house. The loans to friends have never been repaid and the investments are slow to show a return, if any at all. Jim finally comes to his senses when most, if not all, of his inheritance is gone. Then he gets a letter from the IRS. He owes taxes on the inheritance. Jim feels sick to his stomach. His dream has become his nightmare.

In contrast, there is Jane. Jane is an Old Money Gal (*OMG!*), whether by birth or by choice, and she, too, receives an inheritance of one million dollars from her uncle. Jane is also college educated, working, saving what she can, but generally living paycheck to paycheck. And let's not pretend: Jane, too, is ecstatic. *It's a million dollars.* She, too, is ready to party. She calls all her friends, meets them at the local pub, and buys drinks for everybody and has a great time.

But she doesn't mention the inheritance. They're her friends, and friendship is a tremendously valuable thing in life. Sudden changes in circumstances can change relationships—ask any professional athlete or celebrity. Jane is aware of this, and plays off her generosity to a small, unexpected bonus from her job or a small cash gift from a relative. She wants to hold on to her friends now, and take on new ones very carefully.

The next morning, Jane hauls her hungover butt into the office of a certified public accountant. Not a "financial planner," not a stockbroker: a CPA. This CPA may be someone who has done Jane's taxes in the past, or may be a referral from an affluent colleague or family member. This CPA has a roster of clients who have a net worth that is comparable to or exceeds Jane's new net worth. High net worth individuals are nothing new to the CPA; he is probably one himself. The CPA does not need Jane's money. He does not invest Jane's money. Jane sits across from the CPA, explains the inheritance, and asks a very important question: "What is my tax situation?" Then Jane listens very carefully and follows the CPA's advice.

The next thing Jane does...is nothing. Jane has the CPA now as an advisor. The inheritance sits in savings or money market accounts, doing little, but not going anywhere, either. Jane goes back to work at her job and does not mention the inheritance. On weekends, she looks online and in store windows at all the nice things she can now afford to buy. She makes a list of her debts and considers which ones to pay off and in which order. She makes notes about her car, and possible repairs it might need in the near future. She thinks about a trip she might take in the summer. If she doesn't really like her job, she considers what she might do for a living—and maybe make less money—but be happier. She considers the pros and cons of more education, perhaps living abroad. She quietly adjusts to this new financial situation.

Slowly, six months to a year after receiving the inheritance, Jane begins to make financial decisions. She pays off her student loans and her credit card debt. She pays the IRS. She joins a health club whose membership is made up of affluent men and women; she stays healthy and meets new people. She retains the services of a money manager—maybe—who counsels other high net worth individuals. She makes a few conservative investments with a portion of the inheritance. She donates anonymously to a charity that is meaningful to her, and that feels good. Jane has a will drafted by an experienced attorney who specializes in that area of the law. She may establish a trust and hold the majority of her assets in the trust if the attorney, CPA, and money manager agree that it would be wise. Jane, her CPA, her money manager, and her attorney now have one common goal: to minimize Jane's tax liability, protect her inheritance, and increase her net worth over the long haul.

Jane does not buy a big house and an expensive car. She does not create an *unsustainable lifestyle* for herself. Even if she goes off the rails and buys a Rolex or a 96-inch flat-screen television, she's still in good shape overall. She considers what each purchase will cost. Not just what it will cost to *buy*, but what it will cost to *own*. A Rolex watch, once purchased, doesn't cost much to own. Neither does a flat-screen television. But a big house does cost a lot to own. So does an expensive car. Jane knows this and considers it when she spends her money.

Jane also considers the value of what she is purchasing. A meal at a restaurant that costs a thousand bucks and is over within a few hours has a different value than a high-quality winter coat that costs a thousand bucks and lasts a lifetime. Both are luxuries. One just lasts much longer than the other.

These different definitions of value, luxury, and different priorities influence the choices of Old Money (or someone else) when they make purchases or investments. The scenario above and the two contrasting choices made by Jim and Jane reflect the differences in thinking. Jim saw the inheritance as a windfall of money. Jane saw the inheritance as an opportunity.

This made all the difference in how Jim and Jane allocated their resources.

PART I

♦

Core Values

HEALTH

"He who has health, has hope. And he who has hope, has everything. – Benjamin Franklin

The first core value of Old Money is health. You can have millions of dollars in the bank, but if you are not healthy, you are not truly wealthy.

Old Money is active. It eats well, but moderately. It rarely smokes cigarettes and enjoys cigars and pipes in moderation, and almost never in public. The same moderation applies to alcohol.

As we all know, exercise, sport, and leisure activities contribute substantially to good health and aren't necessarily expensive. Walking, running, or taking the stairs instead of an elevator doesn't cost a dime. Regular exercise increases longevity; it provides a boost of energy, a break for the mind, and nourishment for the spirit. Leisure activities expand the social network, encourage friendships, and may facilitate career advancement.

A simple exercise regimen that can easily be done first thing in the morning is to ride a stationary bicycle for 15 minutes to enhance cardiovascular function. Stationary bikes need not be expensive. Used ones are often offered for sale by people who have purchased them new and don't have the discipline to use them. Check your local classified ads.

Include a yoga routine. Yoga does many great things, both physically and psychologically: it decreases blood pressure, increases joint flexibility, improves hand-eye coordination, improves posture and balance, boosts the immune system, and improves the quality of sleep. One simple and easy-to-learn routine is the Five Tibetan Rites. Illustrated instructions can be found online. Buy a yoga mat. Pay cash.

Consider using light weights (5 lb. barbells work well). These can firm up the arms without bulking, which is good for women who like to go sleeveless and men who like to fill out a jacket. The focus is on triceps, biceps, and shoulders, with small weights and more repetitions.

Consult your doctor before starting any exercise regimen.

Diet

Old Money prioritizes healthy living through diet, as well. Most Old Money households eat fresh vegetables and fruit, and lean meats, usually purchased on a weekly basis. Old Money avoids fast food, processed food, and heavy, overly sweet foods, and watches carbohydrates carefully. Carbonated drinks are limited, if consumed at all. Fruit juices, vegetable juices, and filtered water figure prominently. (Brita makes an excellent water filter; get one.) Organic foods or foods grown at home in a garden are not uncommon.

It is rare that an Old Money family will have six months' supply of canned food sitting in the pantry. It's a waste of money and unhealthy. Canned food is devitalized and can be less nourishing. The most nourishing food is the freshest food. The freshest food is the food that has made the shortest journey from the place it is grown to the place it is consumed. If organic food can be purchased from a local farmer at a farmers market, or grown at home, that is best. Food grown in another state or country that has been harvested in large quantities, cleaned, processed, packaged, frozen, stored for who knows how long, then sold in a supermarket is less desirable.

Portions served at mealtimes are moderate, especially at night when no more exercise is likely to occur. A healthy and economical dinner menu for the week might look like this:

- Monday: Grilled breast of chicken, green beans with roasted garlic, yams.

- Tuesday: Pasta with vegetables, including tomatoes, broccoli, bell peppers, and a green salad.

- Wednesday: Grilled salmon, long-grain brown rice covered with black beans, and green peas.

- Thursday: Nicoise salad, light on the tuna and boiled potatoes, heavy on the green beans and tomatoes, with a vegetable soup.

- Friday: Sliced turkey with black-eyed peas, yellow squash, and a green salad.

- Saturday breakfast: A vegetable omelette made with three eggs, bell peppers, onions, olives, and goat cheese; potatoes; and wheat toast.

- Sunday breakfast: A large bowl of polenta (or grits) topped with goat cheese and sautéed mushrooms.

The above items are simple and quick to prepare. Most require only a stove, olive oil, and a few pots and pans.

Note: minimize the intake of red meat, as recent studies link the consumption of red meat to heart disease and cancer. Avoid hamburger meat altogether.

Health and Children

Old Money parents prioritize their children's health above all else. They delay luxuries and even necessities for themselves in order to make sure their children have adequate health care and a nutritious, balanced diet. A family that drives its Mercedes-Benz through the local fast food drive-thru and orders hamburgers and French fries for their children is not Old Money. This behavior is indicative of a family who has its priorities out of order; thus, its resources have not been allocated correctly, and something gets short-changed. It is true that fast food can be cheaper and more convenient, but that's no excuse for eating it or feeding it to your children.

Old Money families also require regular physical exercise from their children, regardless of the children's personality or temperament. It requires only discipline and effort to walk, alone or as a family, at given times during the week.

Because Old Money families watch less television than others, their children perform better in school and are less exposed to the plethora of unhealthy processed foods marketed to children on television. They are also more physically active. Consider limiting your children's television time for their overall health.

Dental Health

Dental health is a priority, as it is critical to overall health as well as to overall appearance. Old Money makes it a priority to see a dentist regularly.

Obviously, cavities and gum disease are minimized with regular brushing, flossing, and visits to the dentist. Chinese medicine, the same philosophy that brought us acupuncture and a number of health-enhancing herbs, links the health of particular teeth with the health of particular organs. While scientific data supporting this may be limited, the case for prioritizing dental health can't be emphasized enough.

In summary, health is key to quality of life. If others depend on you for financial and/or emotional support, you owe it to yourself—and them—to gradually but permanently adopt healthy habits. If for no other reason, realize that unhealthy habits can result in healthcare expenses and cost you money.

Helpful Hints

• Buy groceries for the week, not for the month. This will force you to buy fresh and eat what's on hand.

• Buy fresh vegetables, fruits, grains, and nuts, organic if at all possible. The vegetables are quick to cook (chop, add olive oil, and crank up the stove). The grains (rice) are easy to cook (boil water). The fruits and nuts come in handy in between meals.

• Avoid fast food and processed food.

• Eat small portions of fresh, lean meats. Studies have shown a link between pancreatic cancer and processed meats. Think about it.

• Eat when you're hungry, not just because you're bored.

• Limit commercial television viewing, as it is dominated by food advertising, especially at night.

• Limit sugar intake. Not just in coffee, tea, and desserts, but in all processed foods as well. Read the label. Look at the sugar content.

• Avoid carbonated soft drinks. They're a waste of money and harmful to your health. They rot your teeth and contribute to diabetes, as well as obesity.

• Drinking water in plastic bottles is harmful to the environment and your health, and it's a waste of money. Buy a water filter and carry your own drinking water container.

• Avoid large amounts of coffee. It disrupts sleep and can tax your kidneys. Find a tea you like.

• Cow's milk is expensive and unnecessary for good health. It is a processed food. Avoid it.

• Don't go on fad diets. Don't try to lose weight. Exercise regularly and eat fresh foods. The weight will come off, you won't feel miserable, and you'll live longer.

• Sort out emotional issues, which are often at the core of overeating, by being honest with yourself about things that bother you. Discuss them with a trusted friend or competent professional. Get some answers, make some choices. Move forward without using food as a crutch or a weapon to beat yourself up with.

• Drink red wine with or after dinner. One glass is plenty.

• Avoid manufactured salad dressings. Mix olive oil and balsamic vinegar with a small amount of sugar together to create a light, fresh, and healthy salad dressing.

• Do some research and take the vitamins and supplements that work for you.

• If you think you may have high blood pressure, get tested for a magnesium deficiency.

- Join a gym if it's close to home or office and reasonably priced. Go regularly.

- The important thing is consistency. Exercise first thing in the morning, then the rest of the day is yours.

- Take a day off once a week. Let your body rest.

- Don't work out if you're injured. Let it heal.

For Reference

Bikram Yoga, by Bikram Choudhoury. *Spices of Life* by Nina Simonds. *The Game Changers*, *Forks Over Knives*, and *What the Health*, all documentary films available online.

The Relationship

A medical doctor, a dentist, and an acupuncturist.

Medical doctors generally practice Western medicine, which is based on the diagnosis of disease and its treatment. Treatment generally means prescription drugs and/or surgery. This practice is great if you've had a heart attack. They can save your life, treat your ailment, and get you on the road to recovery. In America, this doctor is an MD.

The dentist, a DDS in America, will clean your teeth at least twice a year, advise you of any tooth or gum problems, and offer options to address any dental health issues that arise. If your funds are limited, a good dentist will offer payment options and work with you, as their primary interest will be your health. If this dentist, or any healthcare provider, agrees to discount or delay payment for services, you must honor your commitment to pay them on time, per the terms of your agreement.

Acupuncturists practice Eastern medicine, which is focused more on health and prevention. While they can also provide cures for some diseases, their focus is to make sure you don't have a heart attack in the first place. Their remedies, which may include the use of acupuncture needles, acupressure massage, and herbs, tend to have fewer side effects than prescription drugs. They tend to look more for the cause of a disease first—often lifestyle issues and stress—and the treatment of its symptoms second. Their work has been proven effective in treating back pain, migraine headaches, and many other illnesses. The acupuncturist is usually an OMD or Doctor of Oriental Medicine, licensed in the state in which they practice.

You need a relationship with all of these healthcare professionals. They should all know that you see all of them; they should both be respectful of the other and be willing to communicate with each other. Any healthcare practitioner who thinks their way is the only way is dangerous and should be avoided.

There are many roads to health, but all of them involve diet, regular exercise, healthy habits, prevention, and a constructive relationship with healthcare practitioners. Prioritize health first.

HEALTH
That Was Then. This Is Now.

When I wrote this chapter in 2013, I had already adopted a plant-based diet for a number of years. Still, I was reluctant to encourage others to become vegetarians or vegans. As I was advocating that Americans break free from the "Buy, buy, buy!" consumer merry-go-round, I thought that one cultural revolution at a time would be sufficient.

My views on this issue have changed. I now encourage others to consider a plant-based diet. The reasons are numerous and obvious. They include health factors, personal economic factors, and global environmental factors.

First, the health factors. Obesity rates among Americans are skyrocketing. 2012 to 2013 saw a 1% increase in adult obesity, according to a Gallup Healthways study. Between 2017 and 2018, the Center for Disease Control estimated the prevalence of obesity had risen from 30.5% to 42.4%, and severe obesity increased from 4.7% to 9.2% among the adult population.

By contrast, a recent *Journal of the Academy of Nutrition and Dietetics* study found that only 9.4% of vegans were obese, and that obesity rates drop as people eat less animal products. According to a recent study by Loma Linda University, vegetarians have been shown to have an overall lower body mass index compared to meat eaters, even if they consume the same number of calories.

You are welcome to eat what you like, but it is important that you know the science behind the choices you're making. It is also important that you know that the beef, poultry, pork, and fish industries spend large amounts of money to fund their own "research," which they then publicize in reputable news outlets in order to make you think that eating meat on a daily basis is necessary and healthy. It is neither. I encourage you to become informed about what you're putting into your body and what you're putting on your family's dinner table. Do some independent, fact-based research. Know that the quality of the meat that is consumed is not the same quality of meat your parents and grandparents consumed.

Eating animals is especially a bad choice in the United States. American safety and health regulations governing the raising, feeding, and slaughtering of animals for human consumption are some of the least stringent and poorly enforced in the world.

I am very proud to call myself an American. Historically, America has played an important, pivotal, and largely positive role in world affairs. But the way in which American companies process food products today leaves a lot to be desired, to say the very least. I say this after living in Europe for four years, where the citizens often have a personal relationship with their butcher or fishmonger and demand that their food be fresh, flavorful, and safe to eat.

Conversely, the statistics on food safety in the US are appalling. The CDC estimates that each year 48 million Americans get sick, 128,000 are hospitalized, and 3,000 die from foodborne illnesses.

In 2018, more than 2,500 tons of raw beef were recalled in connection with a salmonella outbreak. People across 25 states fell ill. In the spring of 2019, more than 11 million pounds of frozen, ready-to-eat chicken strips that may have been contaminated with pieces of metal. Over 2 million pounds of chicken have been recalled in 2020, and the year's not over yet.

Tragically, meat production continued largely uninterrupted during the pandemic. It is estimated that at least 36,000 meat processing and farm workers have tested positive for COVID-19 and at least 116 have died, though accurate totals will probably never be known.

Worker safety and product hygiene issues have always been part of the meat processing industry in America. Celebrated author Sinclair Lewis wrote a groundbreaking book about it entitled *The Jungle* in 1906. Today, labor unions, consumer rights groups, and animal rights activists find themselves fighting the same battle: how to protect workers in the industry, consumers in the supermarket, and animals in the field, especially in this age of COVID-19. To be fully informed, I'd encourage you to visit your local stockyard or slaughterhouse and see for yourself. It will provide an opportunity to, literally, see how your sausage is being made.

Furthermore, it would also be good to remember that processed meat has been categorized as a probable Class 1 Carcinogen by the International Agency for Research on Cancer, a division of the World Health Organization. To avoid confusion, "processed meat" includes the following categories and items:

Lunch meats:	Sausages:	Prepared Meats:
• Ham	• Blood Sausage	• Chicken Nuggets
• Turkey	• Hot Dogs	• Rotisserie Chicken
• Roast Beef	• Summer Sausage	• Fast Food Hamburgers
• Pastrami	• Winter Salami	• Frozen Hamburgers
• Salami	• Pepperette	• Frozen Pizzas (with meat toppings)
• Bologna	• Klobasa	• Pizza Rolls
• Corned Beef	• Extrawurst	• SPAM
	• Vienna Sausage	• Bacon (precooked)
	• Chorizo	• Frozen Dinners
		• Chicken Wings
		• Frozen Chicken Products
		• Corn Dogs
		• Breakfast Burritos

Food for thought, as they say.

In the case of pork, there is always the risk of contracting trichinosis, a disease caused by eating raw or undercooked pig, wild boar, bear, fox, or walrus meat. This allows the parasitic roundworm called *trichinella* to gestate in the intestines of humans, causing diarrhea, abdominal pain, and vomiting. The worm then lodges itself in the muscle tissue, causing swelling around the face and eyes, rashes, and severe muscle pain. It's a real party.

There is also the risk of mercury poisoning when you overindulge in seafood. While no one really knows how or why our fish are now full of so much dangerous mercury, no one is denying the health risks. The March of Dimes, for example, recommends that pregnant women limit their consumption of tuna to six ounces per week in order to prevent fetal mercury exposure that could result in birth defects.

You should also be aware that 50% of the fish consumed in the US today is being raised on fish farms, not caught wild from rivers, lakes, or oceans. Most likely, they're fed corn, just like a cow or a pig, to make them grow bigger, faster. Fish aren't meant to eat corn or corn by-products. As a result of this and the "factory-farm" conditions in which they're raised, they've become more prone to disease and less nutritious for those who eat them, offering less of the omega-3s that we've heard so much about.

If you still want to include animal products in your diet, try to avoid processed meats. The definition of a "processed meat" is any meat that's been cooked, preserved, or otherwise altered from the way it was when it was cut off of the animal.

Get to know a local butcher or fishmonger who can vouch for the quality of the meat, fish, and poultry products they offer. You will pay more for fresher, cleaner meat. It will take more effort to locate it and prepare it properly. It will, however, be worth it in the long run.

We've addressed the health factors. Now let's talk about the economic factors.

The health impact of our bad food rolls over into about $100 billion a year in medical expenses and lost productivity in the US, according the World Bank. They also calculate that this expense and impact is felt most acutely in working class and poor communities. That's the big picture. Now let's look closer to home.

On a personal level, I know from direct experience that it is much more economical to buy groceries and feed yourself if you are not purchasing cows, chicken, lamb, pigs, and fish to consume. I also know that you can eat just as well, enjoying a wide variety of grains such as couscous, bulgur, quinoa, barley, buckwheat, and millet, as well as pastas, rices, cereals, vegetables, legumes, fruits, sauces, and herbs. You will have more energy, digest your food more easily, sleep better, and have more money in your pocket each week. If that sounds like a logical, winning combination to you, then please join me in not eating animals.

Full disclosure: at the beginning of 2020, after a number of years as a vegetarian, I decided to become a vegan. This means that, in addition to not eating animals, I do not eat animal products, like milk, butter, gelatin, cheese, and eggs.

However, three or four times a year I will "fall off the wagon" and enjoy a dessert that has some kind of cream in it. Since becoming a vegan, I feel better than I ever have, and, again, I encourage you to investigate how easy it is to transition to a plant-based diet. For the skeptical, consider "leaning into" a plant-based diet three days a week and go from there.

The final reason causing me to advocate for an animal-free diet is the global impact that beef and poultry processing has on the environment. These industries contribute substantially to global warming. Of course, scientists hired by and lobbyists working for the dairy industry will contest the findings of independent scientists who have been analyzing this problem for years. It would be wise to view their claims with suspicion.

Let me simply offer a thumbnail sketch of the resources required to put a steak on your plate. (I won't even go into putting that fried chicken in your bucket or bacon in your skillet, but the processes are disastrously similar.) First, we're going to need some land on which to raise the cow. A lot of land. We're going to need water for the cow to drink. We're going to have to feed the cow, so we'll need more land to grow crops to feed the cow. It's going to require about seven pounds of feed for you to end up with that 16-ounce steak on your plate. So if you're having dinner for four, and everyone's having a 16-ounce steak, that's 28 pounds of feed used to put the meat on the table for one meal. So we'll need more water, fertilizer, and pesticides for the "feed" part of the process.

We're going to need to be profitable, so we need the cow to grow bigger, faster. We'll add growth hormones (steroids) to the cattle, which you'll ingest when you eat the cow meat, but don't worry about that. There's a chance that these hormones may impact your health, but a good steak is a good steak. When the cow is ready to slaughter, we're going to have to put it in a big truck and drive it to a slaughterhouse. This is going to require fuel, so we need to continue drilling for oil, and there will be carbon emissions from those trucks.

The slaughterhouse that processes the cow is going to contribute substantially to the pollution of our environment. (It's estimated that two-thirds of America's meat processing plants dump massive amounts of nitrogen into rivers and streams each year, in violation of EPA regulations.) Meat processing plants also contribute substantially to greenhouse emissions, about 15% of the total yearly damage to the planet. There will also be plenty of opportunity for the animal product to be contaminated during the slaughter process, from exposure to fecal matter to pathogens to God knows what. Job turnover in these plants is high, so a "skilled workforce" processing your meat is probably not in the cards. These jobs are stressful and dangerous for workers, so many don't stay around for any longer than they have to.

At this point, it's going to be important to understand that we're going to commit all of these resources to an animal that we're going to kill so we can eat it once. That is the opposite of sustainable. And it's not as if we have no other choice. We could opt to *not* kill and eat this animal in this very inefficient, cruel, and toxic manner. Many times we make this "default" choice because we haven't been as informed as we could be about how our food choices impact our planet.

But let's continue, because the meat still needs to get from the slaughterhouse to your grocery store. So another truck is going to transport the finished meat product. This is now going to require paper and plastic products to package it, and refrigerated space in the truck and grocery store to keep it cool until you purchase it. It will, however, look red, juicy, and delicious. Just how much of that beauty is the result of food dye is up for debate.

Finally, you purchase your steak. You take it home. You grill it. You eat it. Perhaps it was delicious. The next day, however, you're going to want another piece of meat for another meal. And all the resources we just itemized will be required again, and again, and again, for millions of consumers, every day of every year, to put meat on the table.

We do have options. In high-tech biorefineries cow manure can be converted to clean energy. Cows, goats, and sheep could be left alive and used to produce butter, milk, or cheese, and fertilize the soil. This is the model that many less wasteful countries and cultures around the world use in their agricultural practices. We could adopt these practices in the United States, as well.

You may want to consider that by 2050 we're going to have to feed 10 billion people every day on this tiny planet. Organizations like the United Nations and the World Health Organization are already advocating for a change in the way we eat. If you have children or grandchildren who are going to inherit this earth, the least we can do is consider what choices we're going to make on a daily basis to leave them a more habitable, healthy planet, and a healthier, more sustainable way of life.

A final note: you can also save even more money if you begin growing your own vegetables. This isn't as labor-intensive or space-demanding as it sounds. Investigate resources available online and in your community. Window gardens and hydroponics are a simple, inexpensive way to get started.

Here are some other health issues to consider...

If you have health issues that Western medicine has been ineffective in treating, you may consider the services of a Qigong Master in your area. Look for established practitioners, satisfied clients, and reasonable fees.

For a great, low-impact cardio workout, consider a personal-sized trampoline for your home or apartment. The "Rebounding" exercises on YouTube presented by Keith MacFarlane and his wife are great. Their easy-to-follow routines can benefit the lymph system and lungs, as well as increase muscle tone and blood flow. (Check with your doctor first.)

A mental health danger that doesn't get as much attention as it should is the constant use of social media. The more time you spend on social media, the more likely you are to be depressed and lonely. That's the conclusion of a 2018 University of Pennsylvania study of 140 college undergraduates who were asked to reduce their use of social media to 30 minutes a day over a three-week period. The students noted decreased levels of anxiety, depression, and "the fear of missing out." They had less worry that their life "wasn't as good as" someone else's life…or rather, the life someone else is projecting online. So, as you improve your physical health through diet and exercise, make sure you're doing the same for your mental health. Limit or eliminate your daily exposure to social media.

Vaping (the use of electronic cigarettes) has come into vogue recently. Many people will tell you that vaping is safe and less of a risk to your health than cigarettes. They are wrong. Cigarettes are, of course, responsible for a litany of diseases. The long-term effects of vaping are unknown at this time, but don't be fooled into thinking that vaping is a healthy, more socially acceptable alternative to smoking. The habit *does* weaken your immune system even more than cigarette smoking. So vaping may not directly give you cancer, but it does make you more vulnerable to other illnesses. Like cigarettes, vaping will also cost you money up front to look cool, even if you have to wait awhile before the health risks are fully known. Be patient, though, they'll be discovered soon enough. In the interim, best not to vape.

Tattoos and piercings have only increased in popularity since the original publication of this book. Medical research is drawing the conclusion that some tattoo inks are toxic. What's more, the ink from some tattoos has been known to compromise MRI results, complicating doctors' efforts to make accurate diagnoses. The ink is also being found in cancerous tumors. The risk of rashes, infections, hepatitis, and other diseases make tattoos and piercings something to avoid.

Toxins aren't just found in tattoo ink. Many beauty products used by women today also contain unhealthy levels of toxic chemicals. Because I feel this information is so important, I'm providing an excerpt (below) from *Old Money, New Woman: How To Manage Your Money and Your Life*, in which

I discuss the dangers in detail. If you wear makeup—or know someone who does—you owe it to yourself to be informed.

Saving Face

The Health Fashion Victim refers to the woman who is victimized by the toxins found in the beauty products she buys and uses. This issue is an enormous one, given the size of the cosmetics industry in the United States. (Recent statistics suggest that American women outspend women in every other country in the world on beauty products.)

As with everything you purchase, it's important to know the "true cost" of owning and using a product. For example, if you buy a yacht, you not only have to pay for the vessel. You must pay for insurance, maintenance, fuel, crew, and a place to dock it. The same issues apply to the acquisition of an exotic car, a serious fur coat, or a piece of jewelry. Steep as they can be, the "true costs" of these purchases are only financial.

With beauty products, we're talking about your most prized possession: your health. So, I'm going to specifically address some of the toxins found in cosmetics sold in the United States in hopes that you become more aware about the "true cost" of some of the choices you make when you purchase beauty products.

Again, these are the costs you pay, not just with the "purchase price" of the product, but the price you pay with your health. According to recent reports, European authorities have banned 1,373 substances from cosmetics sold to European women. The United States Food and Drug Administration has, by contrast, banned only 8 and restricted only 3. (Think about that.) Researchers have linked some of these chemicals to various health issues due to their known or suspected effects on hormones in the human body.

The question you may want to ask yourself is this: if European government officials have banned this many substances from the cosmetics that can be sold to their citizens—most of whom are women and young girls—shouldn't you care enough about yourself and your daughters to investigate, become informed, and ban these same toxins from your life?

Before I discuss in detail the hazards associated with many cosmetics on the market today in the United States, I want to discuss makeup's health effects on our young women and girls. I'll refer to "tweens"—girls between the ages of 10 and 12—and teenagers first.

It's important to be aware that more teens and tweens are wearing makeup than at any other time in history. Sadly, today's American teens and tweens have been brainwashed to believe that they have an "image" to create and maintain. For many, that image includes masking their faces in make-up every day. Many of them absolutely refuse to leave home without it.

Many teenagers in North America have a daily make-up ritual that includes lipstick, powder, blush, foundation, mascara, eyeliner, nail polish, and perfume, not to mention skin lotion, shampoo, conditioner, and hair color treatments. In fact, experts estimate that a typical young girl now walks around with at least a dozen beauty products on her body. As the makeup layers add up, so does her exposure to dangerous chemicals, and that's very bad news for a young girl's health.

Two specific types of chemicals known as parabens and phthalates are found in many cosmetics and have been found to disrupt hormone levels. Since teens tend to use makeup more often, for longer periods of time, and more heavily than adults, they have a greater chance of suffering from health and skin problems early in life as a result of constant exposure to these toxins.

Additionally, peer pressure can often prompt them to cover any blemishes with even more makeup. In turn, this action brings on or worsens acne, creating a harmful cycle of skin damage that may take months or years to reverse. It is truly a vicious cycle.

Will makeup change the way skin appears? Absolutely. Teens and tweens might have a skewed idea of the immediate effect makeup has on their skin, but they may not fully comprehend the problematic correlation it has to skin problems. A recent study in Brazil revealed that 45% of women who used makeup religiously had skin diseases related to the makeup they were wearing.

Makeup can wreak havoc, inflicting damaging and lasting effects on a teenager's skin. As previously stated, the European Union has banned over 1,300 substances from cosmetics sold to European women and girls. Most of the makeup products on the market in the United States actually have some of these 1,300 harmful chemicals in them. Again: researchers have linked these chemicals to various health issues due to the known or suspected effects on hormones. (Think about that.)

Collateral Damage

I think of puberty as a special delight—in retrospect, and for other people. It's a twisting tunnel of change, an emotional roller coaster. Unexpected growth spurts and new, intoxicating emotions keep adolescents who are barely in control of their maturing bodies constantly on edge. All anyone can do is hang on and try to make it through relatively unscathed.

It is a tricky process: you have no warning when it will start, what the ride will be like, or most importantly, when it will end. The young bodies of teens and tweens neck deep in puberty are changing at lightning speed. Luckily, the human body is naturally equipped to handle this turbulent transition. However, many of the chemicals used in makeup can dangerously and unpredictably offset the young body's organic balancing act during this period.

What's more, the manner in which tweens and teens use makeup adds to the health risks. As adult women, you may share your makeup with your "girls" (a little blush here, a touch of mascara, a little extra liner pencil, and just a dab of lip gloss). Generally, though, you carry your makeup. Your friends carry theirs. You know what you're using. It's not a "pass around pack."

However, teens and tweens generally have a much larger circle of friends with whom they share makeup. For the most part they have no idea of how those friends (with whom they are sharing their makeup) are using their own makeup, or who they are sharing it with. Why is this a hazard?

Liquids like primer, foundation, lip gloss, mascara, and their applicator brushes provide a fertile breeding ground for bacteria. Unwitting users then add their own bacteria cocktail from their lips, hands, eyes, and faces. That bottle, tube, applicator brush, or sponge then turns the makeup into a dangerous culprit for a whole host of illnesses and diseases. Unknowingly, teens and tweens often spread harmful bacteria exponentially through shared makeup products. As we discussed, makeup can have annoying and damaging effects on its users, especially developing teens and tweens. Already dealing with skin issues from raging hormones, genes, and germs in the environment around them, the last thing they need are additional makeup-related health issues.

Symptoms like pink eye, staph infections, and those awful makeup-induced acne lesions, medically known as *acne-cosmetica*, can be a result of wearing makeup too soon, too frequently, and too heavily. We all know that teen acne is no laughing matter: for teens and tweens in an often brutal peer-pressure environment, it can make the problems of puberty a thousand times worse. Taking a step back, reassessing the role of beauty products in your life, and defining a new, common-sense approach are key.

The Simple Solution

Many of the known side effects associated with teens and tweens using makeup can be simply and easily resolved. It is your responsibility to create a proper skin care routine— for yourself and your daughters—early in order to develop and maintain beautiful skin naturally. I would suggest that young girls under the age of 16 not wear any makeup at all. When teens do begin to wear makeup, they should take care to use water-based makeup and apply it sparingly with clean brushes.

It is your responsibility to find products free from harmful chemicals that will support a healthy makeup collection. When in doubt about a product or ingredient, do your own research before applying it to your skin.

One great resource is the Skin Deep Cosmetic Safety Database—which you can access at CosmeticsDatabase.com. Just plug in the name of your favorite makeup product and the database will tell you if it contains any known dangerous ingredients.

Again: you must also ask yourself if you know exactly what you're purchasing—the product, and its "true costs" to you and your health—when you buy cosmetics. You're not just getting the benefit of "the look" they provide. You're getting the impact—short and long term—of the health risks they carry. You should also ask yourself this: "Even if I adopt a devil-may-care attitude toward my own health and my own life with regards to cosmetics, what health risks am I exposing my children—born and unborn—to?"

When toxins get into your bloodstream, they don't just stay with you. You pass them on to your child before they're born, and afterward, during the breastfeeding process. Furthermore, if you set an example of purchasing and using toxic cosmetics on yourself, can you blame your daughters for adopting your habits, buying the same toxic products, and using them? Is that really a legacy you want to pass on?

I will tell you this about Old Money Gals: when it comes to their health and the health of their children, they ask a lot of hard questions, and they continue to ask hard questions until they get satisfactory answers. If they don't get a satisfactory answer about a product that may affect their health or the health of their family, it's over: they don't buy the product. They don't allow it in the house. They don't allow their children to use it. They prioritize health over appearance because nothing is more beautiful than a woman with healthy, clean, fresh skin.

Police the people in your head, especially the ones telling you that you must wear makeup to be attractive. Listen to your instincts. Listen to your body. Know that the "true cost" of "beauty" can never be at the expense of your health.

Toxic Relationships

Now, let's take a look at some of the ingredients in cosmetics that victimize women and girls, and the health problems they cause. These substances include:

- **Parabens** - these chemicals have been found to disrupt hormonal levels as they mimic the hormone estrogen and are linked to cancer, reproductive toxicity, immunotoxicity, neuro-toxicity, and skin irritation, as well as increasing the chances of breast cancer. They are found in shampoos and other bath products.

- **Formaldehyde** - found in nail polish and hair treatments, a known carcinogen.

- **"Fragrance"** - this word on a product label can mean anything, as companies aren't required to disclose what chemicals are included. Common toxins include hormone disruptors which con-tribute to breast cancer, among other things. Avoid this by purchasing products scented only with organic essential oils.

- **Coal tar dyes** - banned from food products, but still found in hair dyes, lipsticks, and other products. Look for the *color index* (CI), followed by a five-digit number on the ingredients label, to determine if coal tar dyes are present in a product.

- **Talc** - found in eye shadows, body powders, face powders, and many loose mineral products.

Contributes to ovarian tumors, among other things.

- **Mineral oil** - a petroleum-based product and a known carcinogen. Found in baby lotions, creams, lip balms, and numerous other products.

- **Aluminum zirconium** - found in antiperspirants and linked to the development of Alzheimer's disease, as well as breast cancer.

- **Sodium laureth** - found in a number of different cosmetics, causing skin damage, eye damage, and liver damage. One of the most dangerous unregulated products found in a variety of beauty products (shower gel, exfoliant, liquid hand soap, and toothpaste). Has long been used in industrial cleaning products.

- **BHA and BHT** (Butylated Hydroxyanisole & Butylated Hydroxytoluene) - preservatives widely used by the food industry; also found in a range of cosmetics, these damage the reproductive system and impede proper thyroid function, and can negatively impact other organs as well.

There is an extreme injustice in the fact that many women voluntarily pay exorbitant prices for cosmetics that, first, enrich male-dominated companies, and, second, contribute to a wide range of illnesses, many of them deadly to women. It is easy to avoid being a fashion victim, both in terms of health and finances, when it comes to cosmetics: become informed, purchase healthier, and purchase less.

Another enormous health issue is COVID-19, which ambushed the world in late 2019 and continues to spread around the globe well into the late summer of 2020. It has been a shocking and challenging time for everyone.

My wife and I endured the initial phases of the pandemic holed up in our apartment in Paris, with groceries stacked up against the wall, and no idea what we were going to face. We read the news and talked with neighbors. We also followed responsive, well-thought-out instructions from the French government as they quickly moved to test, isolate, and treat thousands of people at the outset. France was locked down from mid-March to mid-May of 2020. Only trips to the grocery store, pharmacy, doctor, and essential work were permitted. The City of Light became a ghost town. Only after getting control of the virus did the French authorities slowly reopen the country. It was a hard, difficult, and costly process, but it saved lives.

As the routine here returns to some version of "normal," masks are now mandatory. Social distancing is practiced by most of the public, most of the time. Free tests are available to anyone who wants them.

A second wave may visit the country, but as I write, the infection rate is being monitored and the spread controlled. France is slowly coming back, but not without substantial human and economic costs.

In contrast to this experience is the horror we watched unfold in the United States. This disaster has been reported on and recounted ad infinitum, so I won't regurgitate the details here. It is necessary, though, to restate that the virus is highly contagious and deadly. The scope of its long-term health impacts are unknown, but what doctors have seen is terrifying. At present, we don't have a treatment or vaccine.

Therefore, we must be smart.

It's critical that you wear a mask. It's critical that you socially distance. It's critical that you wash your hands. Overall, it's essential that you take this thing seriously and exhibit discipline, caution, and common courtesy. Yes, you have many rights and freedoms in America. You also have a responsibility to act like an adult in the middle of a pandemic, if for no other reason than to honor our healthcare professionals. These doctors and nurses are working day and night, treating coronavirus patients, and sometimes paying the ultimate price—getting sick and dying—while they try to save lives.

This is a war. It does not care that you are tired of it. It shrugs at your desire to go on vacation or hang out with your friends.

Your choices impact your life, the lives of those you love, and people you don't even know.

Be smart. Be careful. Be healthy.

◊ ◊ ◊ ◊

As I mentioned, I'm including in this edition some blog posts from the past six years to inspire and entertain. This one refers, obviously, to health. Enjoy.

From *The Old Money Book* blog
August 12, 2018

Look What I Can Do!

Life gives you a body,
always young and often strong;
You revel in shoulders stretched so broad
and legs striding out so long.

You run like an endless wind,
intoxicated with the new,
You flex and sprint and oft proclaim,
"Look what I can do!"

But little attention is paid
to that Constant Twin in grey
Who matches step for step,
as you frolic, skip, and play.

The Shadow of Time is with you,
each moment and every hour,
And it is greater than anything
you have within your power.

So be kind to your physical self
as you cultivate your mind,
And know that nothing can protect you
from the calendar's daily grind.

For like a serpent coiling slowly,
Time will one day turn on you,
And whisper a familiar exclamation,
"Look what I can do!"

EDUCATION

"Education is not the filling of a pail, but the lighting of a fire."
— *William Butler Yeats*

The second core value of Old Money is education. This may be the most obvious core value, given the general public awareness of Old Money's tendency to send its children to Harvard, Yale, and other such institutions. But the value of education, and the actions that result from it, extends more deeply than that.

Old Money reads to its children from an early age. This strengthens the bond between parent and child. It enlivens young minds. Reading to your child and giving them your undivided attention in a caring manner creates an association in their minds between books and love. This will encourage them to associate books with positive experiences and emotions. The value of this association as they go forward in life cannot be underestimated: how different a world it would be if young people sought answers to life's challenges in the works of great authors rather than in the use of drugs, violence, and alcohol.

Old Money invests time and energy in activities that nourish the intellect and imagination of their children. It takes its children to libraries and on field trips. It eats dinner with them, not in front of the television, and has lively and intelligent conversation. Most importantly, Old Money sets an example by reading more than it watches television. If Old Money watches television, it is PBS.

Old Money will prioritize its children's education by making sure, if private school is not feasible, that their children attend the best public school possible, even if they live in more modest circumstances to make this happen. Other people may buy a nicer home in an area with lower quality schools. Old Money will, if it has to, rent a smaller apartment in an area with better schools. Instead of buying a fishing boat or a new SUV, it will invest in tutors and encourage extracurricular activities to ensure a quality education for its children.

A key to quality education is an early start. Reading, writing, and math skills are developed early. Old Money enrolls its children in rigorous, no-nonsense grade schools and prep schools. Students often wear uniforms to encourage the concept of equality and to remind them that they are students first and foremost. Some are separated by gender to remind them that they are in school to learn, not to socialize. The reality for parents of all income levels and social classes is that it is much easier to parent a child who has been beat over the head all day (figuratively, of course) with challenging concepts and daunting scholastic expectations by a stern, demanding, and passionate faculty. It is also much easier to transition to the rigorous demands of college academia if the student has experienced a rigorous academic experience early on.

The expectation that the children will attend and graduate from college is absolute in Old Money families. This sets the tone for establishing good study habits early. There is very little tolerance for poor academic performance. Extracurricular activities such as sports, drama, music, or debate are encouraged, with very little room for negotiation.

The importance of getting a good education should be communicated to children at the earliest possible age. It should be planned for by parents even before the child is born. Education is fundamental for quality of life, and a common element in upward mobility. Beyond that, it helps one understand society, how things change, and how they never really change. It is essential to learn to do a task, and do it well, even when one doesn't feel like doing it. On a personal level, education gives the educated options, perspective, and a set of tools that, once obtained, cannot be taken away. On a social level, it is essential to the preservation of liberty and the functioning of democracy.

A student who majors in English literature in college may pursue a career in real estate after graduation. That does not mean the college education is wasted. True, certain jobs require a specific college degree. However, the value of an education lies not only in the technical knowledge obtained through study, but in the overall college experience: the introduction to passionate teachers with broader perspectives, the interaction with fellow students from diverse backgrounds, the demands made when digesting more articulate and nuanced intellectual concepts, the terrifying elation that results from having more freedom and more responsibility than ever. At its best, the college experience is the gateway from adolescence to adulthood that broadens the mind and polishes the thinking process. At its most fundamental, it is a time-tested bridge from poverty or limited means to self-reliance, and even prosperity.

Obviously, financial resources make a quality education more accessible, but limited financial resources are no excuse for not securing an education for yourself or your children. Grants, scholarships, and financial aid are abundant.

Education is something to plan, prioritize, and make a reality. For your child, the place to start is with your local public school. If you believe that your child is getting an adequate education at his (or her) present school, consider hiring a tutor to enhance development. The tutor might help in their weaker subjects, or accelerate their understanding of a subject your child really enjoys. If you feel that your child is not getting a quality education, investigate a local Catholic school. The nuns are hell, but the kids learn. Seek out private schools or public schools in other neighborhoods. Don't assume that you can't afford it or that your child won't fit in. Schools can be flexible, and children adapt.

As a point of reference, note this list, by no means comprehensive, of top-tier preparatory schools (preparing students for college) in the United States: Trinity, Horace Mann, and Brearley in New York City; Phillips Academy Andover; Roxbury Latin in Boston; Phillips Exeter and St. Paul's in New Hampshire; Lawrenceville in New Jersey; Groton, Choate, and Milton in Massachusetts; Hopkins in New Haven, Connecticut; College Preparatory School in Oakland, California; and Harvard-Westlake in Los Angeles.

Ivy League universities are the Holy Grail of many ambitious young people and parents who want to enter the upper class and assimilate with Old Money. These schools include Harvard, Yale, Princeton, Dartmouth, Cornell, Brown, Columbia, and Penn. Stanford is a quality school in the western part of the US. These schools are large and offer quality education as well as influential alumni associations. Less well-known, but still very desirable, are smaller colleges including Bard, Fairfield, Williams, Amherst, Vassar and Wellesley (for women), Bowdoin, Holy Cross, Washington and Lee, and Whitman College and Claremont McKenna College in the West.

The lists above refer predominantly to institutions in the northeast of the United States. This is the part of the country settled first by Europeans, and thus, has more history, and, some would argue, more culture, than any other part of the country. The Northeast definitely has a more academic and literate culture than many parts of the country. Boston has been referred to as the Athens of America. The same will never be said of Los Angeles. If you have a choice, get your education (or your children's) in the Northeast.

If that is not possible, identify the best university or college in your area. In this case, "best" means a school that has a strong department in your chosen field of study (for example, Texas A&M has a strong engineering department), and a school with a strong alumni association (being a UCLA or USC graduate in Los Angeles has tremendous advantages, regardless of major). What you learn in school and who you can reach out to when you graduate are key elements of higher education. Strive for excellence in both.

If you are an adult, continuing your education through evening, weekend, or online classes is a great way to enrich your life and learn new skills. Local universities and colleges have much to offer. Investigate.

There are less obvious aspects of education, namely reading and travel, to be discussed in more detail later in this book.

Helpful Hints

Make sure your child gets the best possible education available. Move to a better neighborhood; work an extra job; do without other things. This is a priority above all else.

- Talk to your children. Listen.

- Don't react when they tell you something shocking or unbelievable. It's not the last time you'll hear something shocking or unbelievable from them.

- They have come through you and are being raised by you, but they are not *yours*. They are their own people, on their own paths. Do your best to teach by setting an example and being there for them, but some things they'll just have to learn on their own. As long as these lessons aren't life threatening or potentially permanently damaging, that's okay.

- Don't overparent. Let them learn on their own or from peers or mentors.

- Do not leave your child's education solely in the hands of schools and teachers. You are their first teacher, and their most important. Be involved.

• Make sure your child gets the fundamentals of grammar, spelling, math, and science. Make sure they have structure in their lives and their education. This will ground them and make them feel secure.

• Make sure your child gets the best breakfast possible. Get up earlier. Cook it yourself if you must. A well-nourished child is a better student.

• Don't stifle your child's creativity. That's their joy, their gift to the world. Encourage them to use it productively.

• Be honest about your child. He or she may be more artist than lawyer. Make peace with it. Communicate to your child that you're fine with whatever profession they choose, the only criteria being that it makes them happy and that they do their best. But they still must get an education.

• Develop strong relationships with your child's teachers. Talk to them regularly. They will see behavior in your child that you may never see.

• Eat at your child's school cafeteria. If the food is substandard, pack their lunch.

• Be the home that all the other kids come over to visit.

• Your child has friends. Know their parents. Forge a strong relationship with those parents who share your values.

• Know what your child is learning. Or not learning. Postpone buying a new car; hire a tutor to button up your child's weaker subjects.

• Encourage your child to learn more about something of particular interest to them. Support their passions.

• Limit television, computer, and mobile phone screen time at home. Know what websites your child is visiting. Know who they're talking to online. Studies have shown that intelligence decreases as television viewing time increases. It's not a coincidence.

• Video games are a waste of money and a brain drain. Limit your child's exposure to them.

• Require your child learn a second language. Start early. Learn it yourself. Start speaking it at home. Make the process fun. Invite neighbors or colleagues who speak the language fluently to your house. Have them speak to your children. A new language is a new world.

• Make sure your child learns to play a musical instrument. It will increase their intelligence and put them in touch with their emotions. Investigate music programs like *El Sistema* in your area. They offer musical instruments, lessons, and orchestra training to students of all socio-economic backgrounds.

• Take your children to the library regularly. Read to them early in life. Encourage them to read books about whatever interests them. Ask them about what they're reading. Nourish their minds. Set an example. Read worthwhile books.

• A library of worthwhile books in a home is a treasure. There's no need to pay retail for books. Thrift stores sell books, and used books are available online. Book fairs are great events for parents and children. Ask a librarian for a list of classics that form the basis of a good library. If you child has read these before they are introduced to them in school, they're ahead of the game.

• To get your son to read the Bard, tell him chicks dig Shakespeare (wink, nod).

• If possible, take your children on vacations and short trips with family members only. Strengthen the family bond. Make the family unit the most important peer group your child has. Give them a sense of belonging; they will be less likely to seek it from undesirable sources outside the family. Isolating your children in this manner for a period of time makes it more difficult for them to hide things from you. It also makes them think twice about doing something to disappoint the family.

• If you screw up in front of your kids, admit it. If possible, laugh at yourself.

• If you notice a radical change for the worse in your child's behavior, get in their face and stay there until you get an answer about what's wrong. Be supportive, but be firm.

• You may or may not spank your child on the bottom or hand while they are an infant, but you cannot hit a child of any age for any reason. If you suspect another child of being abused, call the local police and social services. Making two reports reduces the opportunity for child abuse to slip through the cracks.

• Teach your child to handle money, alcohol, and sex. Managed correctly, all three contribute generously to the enjoyment of life. Mishandled through ignorance or neglect, disaster looms. Be blunt, honest, and available to answer questions. Conversations can be awkward, but negligence is far worse.

Think about all of the above before you decide to have children. If you already have children, good luck.

For Reference

• Your local public library. Secondhand bookstores. Book fairs.

• Rosetta Stone and online language resources.

• Museums. Museums offer incredible and often under-used educational resources. Take a Saturday and go.

• Take your children. Explore.

• Documentary films and public television programs that offer insights into subjects that interest you.

The Relationship

Tutors. Help your children by helping them with challenging subjects. College students are often available to tutor at very reasonable rates. They also can be great role models.

Librarians. These unsung heroes know books and they know children. They've seen a lot of both come through the door. Befriend them. Introduce your children to them. They can be a good influence on your children and an ally to you.

EDUCATION
That Was Then. This Is Now.

The acquisition of a quality education is a cornerstone in building an enduring quality of life. Nothing has changed in this regard.

While the cost of college tuition has increased substantially over the past 10 years, the value of a college education remains. In 2018, the US Bureau of Labor Statistics estimated that college graduates with bachelor's degrees earn a median weekly salary of $1,172 to just $712 for those with only a high school diploma. Other estimates indicate that a college graduate will normally earn more than $600,000 more during their careers than those without a college education.

When I refer to "value," I'm not only referring to the ability to make more money. College graduates have lower divorce rates, better health, and longer lifespans than their less educated counterparts.

Yes, I realize that student loan debt is a very real thing and that job opportunities may be shaky during and after this pandemic. An education is still worthwhile. It is still worth the sacrifice and the work.

It is essential that you receive an education in order to better understand your world, especially during these (seemingly) unprecedented times. You will have a better perspective, a better technical, psychological, and emotional "tool box" with which to process information, filter out BS, and maximize opportunities if you expose yourself to the college experience.

It is a reality, right now, as I write this, that online classes may be necessary to ensure the health of students and faculty. But don't fall into the comfort zone of thinking that an online education is the same thing as the college experience. The atmosphere and the energy of a college campus, as unfamiliar, chaotic, and challenging as it can be, is part and parcel of your education. You need to meet new people, participate in the school's traditions, get lost on your way to class, endure dorm food, fall in love, study all night, and share the communal, exhilarating, and sometimes nauseating rollercoaster ride of being a freshman at college. At the end of it all, you will have the satisfaction of being a college graduate. And while the world may not be your oyster at the end of this process, it will most certainly be broader, richer, and more manageable.

Education is the bridge that takes you from being a snotty-nosed teenager into adulthood. Do not be fooled by journalists who write articles casting doubt on the value of a college education. They are probably college graduates themselves who work for editors who are, I'm certain, college graduates, at a newspaper or online publication that is, I'll bet you, owned by a college graduate.

If you doubt the transformative power of an education, watch the documentary series *College Behind Bars*, currently available on Netflix. It is the story of prison inmates in upstate New York who are given the opportunity to get a college education from visiting Bard College professors. You will see convicted felons who viewed their lives in very limited terms blossom into articulate, thoughtful, and polished young men and women with bright futures. Prepare to be astonished at their change in attitudes, vocabulary, demeanor, and character. This, dear reader, is the impact of a quality education.

If going to college is not in the cards for you because of your personal situation, age, or vocational inclination, a priority for you may be to become licensed, certified, or bonded

61

by trade organizations or public agencies that regulate your profession or industry. Your education may be to become a certified welder, licensed beautician, registered nurse, or pilot. These occupations focus on the acquisition of a particular skill set rather than a broader academic background. Still, they ensure that you have a viable way to earn a living, take care of yourself and your family, and contribute to society.

If you are the parent of a young child, you already know that the pandemic has turned the school year—and the educational process—upside down. The structure and social engagement so critical to elementary, junior high, and high school education has been disrupted. It's not possible for teachers to engage the students as effectively online, regardless of their passion for a subject or the wonders of modern technology. I am sure that students and parents alike have suffered.

This may be a moment to sit down with your child and articulate the importance of an education. I am certain it is the time to listen to their concerns, challenges, and fears as they face another uncertain school year.

As you face these challenges, remember this: in the poorest parts of the world right now, parents are working day and night, saving every penny they can, doing without clothing and even food for themselves, in order to give their children an education.

Why? Because in hand-to-mouth economies getting an education is often the difference between life and death. It is the difference between living in a dirt floor hut with no indoor plumbing and actually having a home with electricity. It is the difference between a lifetime of back-breaking manual labor in a field and the opportunity to experience a world of opportunity.

If those parents can do that for their children under those circumstances—circumstances that the pandemic has only made worse—we can certainly be resourceful enough to educate our children during this difficult time.

As I said, a college education may not be for everyone or available to everyone. But the development of a skill set—through education of some kind—is within everyone's reach. We can all put ourselves in a position to function in society, support ourselves financially, contribute to the community, and participate in democracy.

And unlike so many other assets, an education can never be taken away from you once you have it.

THE WORK ETHIC

"If people knew how hard I had to work to gain my mastery, it would not seem so wonderful at all." – Michelangelo

The third core value of Old Money is hard work.

Old Money realizes that there's no good chance at happiness without purposeful, productive work. Obviously, in many cases, Old Money doesn't work because it needs the money. It works because there's joy in doing what you love. Whether it's a profession that provides a paycheck or volunteer work for a charity, Old Money works. All of the world's religions advocate the concept of *being of service*. So does Old Money. Go figure.

There's no comfort in relaxation if you haven't experienced the contrast of challenging work. Old Money has the distinct privilege of often being able to do what it is passionate about for a living. This is born out of Old Money's innate sense of the importance of making a contribution: to oneself, by using God-given talents in a meaningful vocation; to one's family, by producing an income, setting an example for children, and honoring the efforts of parents; and to the community, by creating jobs, and making the world a better place to live.

Old Money discovers what it loves to do, and does that for a living. You should, too. Yes, a good income is wonderful, but if you work at a job you hate—there won't be enough money in the world to make you happy. Confucius' comment about finding a job you love and never having to work a day in your life is as true now as ever.

Old Money is happier, even with less money, and probably in line to make more money at its true calling precisely because it is not doing it *for* money. Money is generally a by-product of doing what one loves—and not surprisingly, what one is good at—and offering that product or service to the world.

It requires courage and a strong sense of self to recognize, accept, and pursue one's true calling. But it is essential to living a full life. It is never too early or too late to discover it and embrace it.

It is also essential to excel at one's chosen vocation, regardless of its potential financial rewards or perceived status in society. Old Money *gets after it.* This work ethic is instilled at an early age. Old Money grows up around achievers who have a strong sense of the privilege they've been born into and the responsibility that comes with it. That responsibility precludes laziness, half-hearted efforts, or just getting by.

Rigorous prep school curricula develop good study habits early. Athletics forge self-discipline. Reading and travel round out character and intelligence. A keen sense of self may be accompanied by a cavalier disregard for convention, but the work ethic is there.

Old Money saying: get your butt in gear.

Inspiration and direction can be found in notable examples of the Old Money work ethic. Born to privilege, author and designer Edith Wharton was a world class OMG (Old Money Gal). She traveled and worked ferociously. She wrote numerous novels, essays, and articles while designing her formidable house in Lenox, Massachusetts, as well as the gardens that surround it. In an era when women of her class did not have careers, especially not as a writer, she ignored such nonsense: she wrote, won a Pulitzer Prize, and lived a rich life.

Theodore Roosevelt set a standard for Old Money behavior throughout his life, writing 35 books, committing himself to progressive causes and public service as president of the United States for two terms, and leaving a truly impressive legacy that primarily benefited America's poor and the working classes. He said his motto was to lead "a life of strenuous endeavor," and so he did.

A few years later, Franklin Roosevelt did likewise, guiding America through the Depression and World War II as its longest-serving president, accomplishing much from a wheelchair, as he had lost the use of his legs to polio (disabled, maybe; discouraged, never.) Part of FDR's charisma and effectiveness as a leader rested in the fact that he tended to treat everyone with courtesy and respect, regardless of their station in life. Again, much of his work was aimed at benefiting the poor and working classes.

All of these individuals were born into wealth and privilege. None of them wasted their lives in the hollow pursuit of pleasure or the gauche acquisition of material things. Note that neither of these presidents leveraged their political power to benefit the moneyed class from which they came, unlike some who have followed them in office.

The Value of Time

A marked characteristic of Old Money is that it does not waste time. This does not mean Old Money does not enjoy leisure. It does. This does not mean Old Money is always in a hurry. It rarely is. What it means is that Old Money knows the value of time and is aware that you cannot bank or borrow it like you can cash. You're going to spend it, one way or the other, and when it's spent, it's gone forever.

Old Money is often focused on *maximizing the moment*, whether it's being productive at work or being joyful at home. Maximizing the moment means committing to what you're doing, without distraction, for the time that you're doing it.

The biggest enemies of this are mobile phones, emails, the internet in general, and television in particular.

If you're going to write or read an email, do it. If you're going to watch a television program—as opposed to sitting down and lethargically watching television for no particular reason—watch it. If you're going to have a conversation with a friend, have it. But don't try to do all three at once. Something will be lost, not the least of which will be the magic in maximizing the moment.

Multi-tasking, a term Old Money loathes, is often just pretending to do more than one thing at a time and doing none of them well. Focus on a task, activity, or person. Invest fully. You will be more productive at work and have more fun when you play.

Self-Discipline

Old Money knows that so much of life depends on the ability to do what needs to be done, when it needs to be done, whether you like it or not. Indeed, this may be the major lesson in all of formal education.

Old Money knows that exercising self-discipline early in life or early in a task makes for much smoother sailing later. While it is not natural to start and finish necessary—and sometimes unpleasant—work that could be put off to a later time or not done at all, it is an important habit to adopt.

It's also best to have goals for different areas of your life, not just your career or finances. Old Money leads a balanced life, and so should you. Goals help develop discipline and give purpose to life. Start small. Conquer your closet before you take on the world. If you did not get the benefit of self-discipline from school or athletics, start with small daily or weekly targets on an area of your life you want to improve. Avoid the pointless; have a definite purpose in mind when developing a habit. Make your first goal so easy you could do it without even trying. But do it. Reach your first goal. Acknowledge your success. Then set your second goal that is a little more demanding. Reach it. Acknowledge your success. And set another goal.

Be brutally honest with yourself about the effort and resources it will take to reach a goal. Don't pretend. If you set a goal and don't make the effort to achieve it, ask yourself why. Most of the time, the reason is lodged in some self-esteem issue. It is the work of life to take the circumstances of our birth and issues of our childhood and discard, refine, and remake them in order to become the person we want to be.

Targeting short-term, accessible, tangible goals that align with a long-term dream or vision you have for your life, and working toward them consistently, is a formula for happiness and accomplishment. It's been said before but bears repeating: it's not the achieving of your goals that will be the true success, but the person you become in the process.

Success is feedback: you did everything correctly, or you did not set your goals high enough. Could you have done more? Congratulations. Get busy.

Failure is feedback: you did not do everything correctly, or you did not work hard enough. Learn from it. No whining. Get busy.

Helpful Hints

• Find a role model in the profession to which you aspire. Look at the road they took to get there. See if it holds any answers for you.

• Find a mentor. This person may be doing what you want to do for a living, or may have advised others in your chosen field on how to proceed. Listen to him. Take his advice.

• What is it that you're doing when time stands still and time flies, all at the same time? What activity puts you "in the zone"? Can you do that for a living?

- What are you naturally good at doing?

- What would you look forward to doing every morning if you didn't have to earn a living? If the answer is what you're doing right now for a living, congratulations. You are one of the lucky few.

- Don't think about working an eight-hour day or a ten-hour day. Focus on working for 45 minutes at a time, addressing whatever task is at hand, without interruption or procrastination. Then take a break if you can. Then go back to work for another 45 minutes. You'll get more done in less time.

- Know the requirements of your chosen profession and exceed them.

- If you start it, finish it.

- If you tell someone you're going to do something, do it.

- "It's not worth it" often means "I'm not worth it."

The real competition is to do better than you've ever done before. And then to do better than that.

When you work hard at something, you honor the task and you honor yourself.

For Reference

The Pathfinder by Nicholas Lore. *Do What You Are* by Paul D. Tieger and Barbara Barron-Tieger.

The Relationship

A Mentor. Someone who is doing what you want to do for a living or has advised other successful people in your chosen profession is invaluable as you pursue your career.

Colleagues. No one succeeds in a vacuum. Colleagues offer support, referrals, and resources. Cultivate them. Offer to help them before asking for help from them. Offer often, ask seldom.

THE WORK ETHIC
That Was Then. This Is Now.

In a post-pandemic world, you will most likely be required to offer more as an employee, business owner, or service provider in order to see the same rewards in terms of salary or profits.

That's a fairly natural consequence of a financial crisis: the market becomes more competitive. Customers get tight with their money. Companies get nervous about their payroll. Everyone wants more, so they can get ahead, but they want to pay less, so they can hold onto their cash. Employees and vendors often have to become more productive and more innovative in order to keep their jobs, retain their clients, and continue to survive, if not prosper.

This often brings forth great inventions and brilliant ideas into society and into the marketplace. It also brings out the ruthless nature of disreputable businesspeople who look for any opportunity to pay workers less and charge customers more.

As you work hard—and harder—you're going to have to be aware of this behavior while maintaining your own integrity, both as a boss and as an employee. This is a time to take advantage of opportunities, not people.

But let's look at the positive side, namely, how you can be more valuable to everyone you work with. Obviously, there are at least two books a week being released by business titans and sales gurus breathlessly detailing how they created value, won customers, and became successful. Great. You can filter through those as you wish.

I will speak to you from experience—the experience of the client or customer here in Paris—in order to offer you simple insights into how this culture excels in the art of service. Perhaps some of these examples can shape our work ethic and performance as we engage with our colleagues and customers.

First, there is the routine of entering a neighborhood café. If it's your first time or your fifty-first time to enter the café, your presence will be acknowledged, and you will be greeted with a sing-song, "Bonjour!" from at least one of the staff, and usually several.

Regardless of how busy or quiet it is, your needs will be almost immediately addressed. "Are you here to eat or just have a beverage? Is it just you or are you meeting someone? Do you want to sit at the counter? Or would you like to take this table?"

If your French is not great, they will try to speak to you in English. The service will be crisp, prompt, responsive, but not overbearing. These professionals work in the service industry. They are not servants. You may be as demanding as you wish, but you may not be rude. They require respect, and in turn offer you their best.

By your third visit, they will know how you like your coffee and where you prefer to sit. They will not share their life's story with you, but they will listen patiently as you re-count your adventures in their city.

This keen, at-the-ready service is omnipresent here, whether you're poised to spend five euros on an espresso or five thousand on a suit. If you do venture into the gilded halls of luxury shopping or hospitality in Paris, be prepared to enter another world. When you enter an establishment, whether it be a boutique or a hotel, you will be greeted by welcoming staff. They are not looking at their mobile phones or grumbling about the bad morning they had at home. They are doing their job: paying attention to you, and making sure that from the moment you enter, you begin to feel valued and appreciated, not marginalized or unwelcome.

I recently had a delightful experience at a well-known men's clothing store. I entered and was greeted with the *bonjour* I've now come to enjoy so much. "How can we help you today?" I was asked. I explained, and the salesperson immediately introduced me to Elizabeth, who had experience in the product I had come to purchase.

Elizabeth introduced herself. She asked if this was my first time in their store. (It was.) Would I be interested in something "off the rack" or bespoke? (Bespoke.) "Ah, right this way." Up we went in a private elevator to the next level (literally and figuratively). Elizabeth detailed the various services that were offered, and invited me to browse through a labyrinth of fabrics. "Would you like something to drink?"

"Water would be fine. Thank you."

"Perfect. Please feel free to explore our collection, and I'll be right back."

Elizabeth soon returned with my Evian, and the fabric selection began in earnest. Once I had selected a candidate, Elizabeth asked me to follow her. She would provide me with some pricing information. She opened a book and explained the range of costs that I might encounter. There was no pressure, no hesitation, no tension. She had taken all the anxiety out of this part of the process by simply anticipating how a customer might feel as they entered this store—and encountered this level of quality, craftsmanship, and service—for the first time.

A fitting followed. Vincent the tailor was introduced, and then a polite but focused line of questioning followed. They were not interested initially in trying to fit me for a shirt and take my money. They were interested in understanding the history and feelings about the shirts I had owned in the past.

They wanted to understand me first. "So, what brings you to us today?" "Do you have to dress for work?" "How do you normally dress? Casual? Formal?" "How would you like to dress?" "Are you physically active when you wear dress shirts?" "How often do you travel? And how do you dress when you travel?"

Only after they had a fairly good understanding of me did the conversation turn to shirts. "Do you have collar and cuff preferences?" "Do you like this fit in the torso?" "Will you be able to return for a second fitting?" "How did your previous shirts wear?" "Did they become too tight too soon?" "Are the shirts we're making for you to wear at work?" "Will we be making this shirt for casual occasions or dress occasions?"

Throughout the entire process, it was my feelings, my interests, my preferences, and my tastes that were sought out, noted, and applied to the job at hand.

As a customer, I was sold. I was a believer. And when I selected a collar style, and Elizabeth hesitated before saying, "Of course, Mr. Tully," I stopped. I asked her what her thoughts were on the collar style, and she replied evenly, "I think it's a little overbearing."

It could have been a tense moment. But it wasn't. Why? Because this team of artisans had taken the time to get to know me, to understand my life, to ask questions, to answer questions, and to make my shirt exactly to my specifications down to the very last detail. So, when they raised a concern, I was all ears. I was listening. I, too, wanted the best, and I wasn't insecure about being wrong because they'd put me first.

I turned to both Vincent and Elizabeth and said, "You've seen a lot of clients, many with a face and frame similar to mine. Which collar would you suggest?" They presented two options. I went with the first one.

And when my final shirt was delivered, I realized: they were right. I had the perfect collar.

I also had the perfect customer experience. Because of their commitment to excellence. Because of their work ethic. You see, "work ethic" not only refers to working hard, paying attention to the details, and following through; it also includes how you want to make people feel when they're doing business with you.

There's also the other end of the stick when it comes to customer service. I've had the short end of that, too. Before my writing career took off, I was working as a busboy at the Hard Rock Cafe in Los Angeles. In the middle of this boisterous and always-crowded restaurant on a Friday night, a woman changed her baby's diaper at the table. If that wasn't bad enough, she handed me the dirty diaper as I walked past, asking if I could "take care of this." After a split second of shock and disdain, I nodded, took the diaper, and made a beeline for the dumpster in the loading dock while trying to hold my breath. It's an example of how not to treat people who are working with you or for you.

Sadly, anyone who's ever worked in the service industry—especially restaurants and bars—can share plenty of stories like this. The point is: you want to endeavor to be the most thoughtful service provider, and the most thoughtful client.

◊ ◊ ◊ ◊

The work ethic is a given in Old Money culture, and its absence is often bluntly called out, as you'll soon read below. It doesn't matter how Old or how Money someone is, they need to be working. This conversation I had with an Old Money Guy in Paris a few years ago will give you an idea of how important the work ethic is. It's brief, enlightening, and entertaining.

From *The Old Money Book* blog
Sept. 26, 2017

OMG Conversation

Recent conversation with an OMG about another. No friendship was going to happen, and the reason was stated with typical Old Money candor:

"So you met him?"

"I did."

"What did you think?"

"I don't get the impression he does anything."

"I think he's just clipping coupons right now."

"Yeah, and I don't like that. We can all do that, but we don't do that. Lack of character. Lack of duty. Not to mention the example it sets for the kids."

"I thought you two would hit it off. Sorry."

"No, not a big deal. We have a lot in common, but there's something missing with the guy. It's a flaw, is all I can say. And frankly, I don't want to be around when idle time hatches some bad behavior. And it's only a matter of time with him, or anybody. And what do you have to talk about if you're not working? Another drink?"

"Sure. (Long pause.) You know I'm working, right?"

(Laughter.) "You're a writer. We're never sure about you guys." (More laughter.)

ETIQUETTE &
MANNERS

"Life is short, but there is always time enough for courtesy."
– Ralph Waldo Emerson

Politeness is the fourth core value of Old Money.

Coco Chanel is rumored to have said that etiquette is for people who don't have manners. She might be implying that manners are common sense, and etiquette is the more technical aspect of doing things properly. You may not know which fork to use at a formal dinner, but if you're well-mannered, you may be forgiven. However, if you lack humanity, no amount of formal training in etiquette will help.

Manners are incredibly simple and, on the whole, based on common courtesy and common sense, which, ironically, are not so common. They only require practice and the awareness—which may come as a shock—that you are not the center of the universe. Try to be a lady or a gentleman and treat others politely even in the most difficult of circumstances. It is a gift that costs nothing and makes the world an infinitely better place. It makes you a better person. It is also a social clue to Old Money that you are one of them, or aspire to be.

You will never be or be near Old Money for long if you are rude or lack manners. There are numerous books available which discuss manners and etiquette in detail. Purchase one and read it frequently, regardless of what you think you know.

Note: Old Money is never condescending to others, regardless of their social position or vocation.

One of the most challenging obstacles to a civilized society today is the use of mobile phones. They are the cigarettes of this generation: they are used by many, often annoying, and will, in time, be known to be hazardous to your health.

Of course they are convenient, and they do enable business to be done at any time and almost any place. But that does not mean that business *should* be done at any time and almost any place. And frankly, most people aren't doing business when they talk on the phone or text at the dinner table. They are not saving lives when they take a call during a face-to-face conversation or meal, or during any other time when common courtesy or common sense dictates that their entire attention should be focused on the task at hand. Such as...driving a car.

The illusion that portable devices promote is that the owner is so important, his or her business so vital to national security (wink, nod), that it is imperative that he or she be in constant communication with...whom? You are not that important. Unless you are on call as a paramedic, fireman, law enforcement officer, or surgeon, your work is not that important.

Spend more time with people who are important to you, face-to-face, talking, listening, laughing, and exchanging ideas with your phone turned off. The world will not end. The likelihood that anything traumatic or life-changing can or will happen during the time you have your phone turned off is miniscule. If something does happen, the timeframe in which you learn about it will, in all probability, make no difference. If you must, contact the person or persons most important to you prior to turning your phone off and tell them you will be unavailable. There is a high probability they will not care. Then turn your phone off.

The effect this will have is twofold: it will flatter the person you are spending time with, and it will relax your mind and enable you to really enjoy and engage with that person. In truth, this is what politeness always does: it makes other people feel good and makes their interaction with you more enjoyable and productive. Furthermore, it costs you nothing and can bring enormous rewards, both personally and professionally.

Manners have been elevated and refined throughout the ages by medieval knights and Renaissance courtiers into "codes of behavior," which dictate behavior regardless of circumstances. The closer you get to defining and adopting your own code that you live by, the closer you will come to being the perfect gentleman or the perfect lady.

Old Money saying: if you know the rules, you can get in the club. And the first rule is manners.

Manners and Children

It won't do you any good, however, to be the perfect lady or the perfect gentleman if you have children who swing from a vine. One of the most demanding tasks a parent has is teaching children manners, but it can be done and must be done, the earlier the better. Children are naturally energetic, spontaneous, and joyful. No one wants to dampen their spirit. They must function in society, however, and learning manners is a big part of that.

Children, for the most part, will learn more from watching their parents than they will from a thousand lectures. It's a harsh reality that most parents learn too late, many times when they see abhorrent behavior in their offspring and ask, "Where on earth did they learn that?" (they learned it from you, dear). So, parents, mind your manners. Little ones are watching.

Another fundamental to instilling good behavior into the young is to explain manners and the reasoning behind them, as children are known to perpetually ask, "Why?" So take the time and explain.

Please note that Old Money children do all the embarrassing, wicked, and panic-inducing things other children do. They just don't do them in public. This allows Old Money parents some peace of mind while they are with their children in public, and it also allows them to actually enjoy family time in public.

Behavior in public restaurants is critical. A strategy to ensure proper behavior by children in restaurants is to rehearse going to a restaurant at home, prior to going out. Schedule family time on a weekend when everyone is not so busy. Explain to the children that the family is going to rehearse going to a restaurant so that everyone will know what behavior is expected, and what behavior is unacceptable.

Everyone will dress appropriately. One of the parents, if there are two parents, will play the role of the host or hostess at the restaurant, as well as the waiter or waitress. The other parent will play the role of the patron who is accompanying the children. The family will be welcomed to the restaurant, seated, and handed menus (have the children write them up; they'll enjoy it and feel included). The "waiter" or "waitress" will take their orders, with each member of the family ordering for themselves, including *please* and *thank you* as they do. The meal will be served and eaten (allowing the waiter or waitress to take a break, be seated, and eat with the family). Conversation will be conducted at a reasonable volume. Napkins will be in laps. Elbows will be off the table. Neither tantrums nor food will be thrown. The meal will be concluded and, if the children have behaved well, a small, appropriate reward will be given.

The children will be gently reminded that this is the way they behave in public. In the privacy of their own room or backyard, they may jump, laugh loudly, or play in the mud and scream like maniacs until their heart's content, or until the neighbors complain (wink, nod). But in public, different behavior is required. Once children know what is expected, when it is expected, and why, they are more likely to adhere to rules, especially if they have designated time to still be children.

Take the time. Teach your children manners. Be persistent. Set an example. Loud, unruly, and poorly behaved children are not cute. They are not adorable. They are not "just being kids." They are annoying.

Manners at Home

Old Money knows that it's important to not only be polite to friends, colleagues, and strangers, but to family members as well. Perhaps it is most important to be polite to family.

At home, Old Money says good morning and good night. It offers to help if someone's cooking a meal. Old Money is dressed; no walking around in boxer shorts with no shirt on, thanks.

When a meal has been prepared, Old Money is courteous enough to show up at the dinner table on time, neatly, if casually, dressed. Old Money doesn't text, play games, or answer emails or calls during a meal.

The family meal is a time to bond, to discuss the progress of everyone's life, to support and encourage, and to laugh. Although serious issues can be discussed, emotional or unpleasant topics should be addressed away from the dinner table.

Napkins are in laps. Food is eaten slowly and enjoyed. The television is not on. The radio is not on.

When the meal and conversation are concluded, the chef—whether it's staff or a family member—is congratulated and thanked. Family members excuse themselves, and often clean up after themselves.

Old Money children may be neat or they may be disorganized, but they have generally been taught to understand that while staff may do their laundry and change their linens, the condition of their room is largely their own responsibility. Old Money children and adolescents keep things generally in order. They must study. They have friends over. Standards must be met.

Television is watched in a particular room, often alone or with members of the family who gather to watch a specific program. If an important conversation needs to happen, the television is turned off or the participants in the conversation go to another room.

Generally, manners contribute to the Old Money home, making it a relaxed and civilized environment where children and adults alike can feel safe, welcome, and supported.

> Note: Old Money does not have affairs with the staff or the employees, as they might not feel they're in a position to refuse, which is not fair. And if the help is making the moves on their employer, well, let's just say that their ambitions are misplaced, and potentially dangerous.

Helpful Hints

- If you are a man, hold the door open for others when you enter a building. Hold the door open for a lady or child when they get into a car.

- Say thank you more often. Use thank you notes. Emails and text messages are not sufficient.

- Do not talk with your mouth full.

- Do not speak or laugh loudly in public.

- Smile. (Ladies, use good judgment with this one in public, as not to be misunderstood.)

- When at a restaurant, do not order the most expensive thing on the menu if you are not paying the bill. It is fatiguing to those of us who do pay the bill.

• Keep your elbows off the table. Sit up straight. Sitting up straight is most easily done by sitting and pushing your butt against the very back of the chair.

• Put a napkin in your lap. Do not slurp your soup or coffee. Eat slowly. Chew your food with your mouth shut, please.

• Wipe your mouth with your napkin, even if you don't think you need to. This is preferable to having someone else inform you that you actually do need to.

• Bring the food from your plate to your mouth. Do not lower your mouth toward the plate.

• Do not point with your fork. Do not point at all.

• Speak clearly; don't mumble. Listen twice as much as you talk. Ask questions.

• Have something interesting and intelligent to talk about. Do this by reading books, newspapers, and generally having a life.

• If necessary, get a life.

• Do not complain. Do not gossip. Do not boast.

• If you are a man, never, ever abandon a woman who may be in danger, regardless of the situation. Come to her defense.

• If you are a woman, never, ever allow a man to be accused or humiliated unjustly by others. Come to his defense.

• Do not discuss sex outside the bedroom. Do not discuss illness outside the family. Do not discuss money unless it pertains to a business transaction.

• Never, ever discuss the amount of money an individual or family has, including yourself and your family.

• Do not tell vulgar or racist jokes. Do not use profanity.

• RSVP means *répondez, si'l vous plait*. That means, in English, "Please respond." This means please reply in a timely fashion to the host or hostess of the event to which you've been invited. Do it, or risk not being invited to future events.

• Gentlemen, treat her like a lady. Ladies, do not go out or have sex with a man who is not a gentleman.

• Everybody, breath mints.

For Reference

Emily Post's Etiquette. This book is your best bet. Buy it. Read it. Refer to it.

Social clubs offer adolescents and young adults the opportunity to learn manners and social skills in a safe environment. Investigate those in your area.

Barclay Classes, for children, if you live in the Northeastern United States. The Etiquette School of the South, Fayetteville, Georgia. The Los Angeles School of Etiquette.

* The American School of Protocol, ATL
* New England School of Protocol, MA

The Relationship

You may wish to consult an etiquette expert in your area. Many teach classes. Consider getting a group of friends together for a session. It's fun and may reduce the price.

There's nothing like going to the source, though. Old Money members of your community may be flattered that you'd ask their thoughts and advice on etiquette. Most of them feel, with some justification, that the world is going to hell in a handbasket and may welcome your help in stemming the tide.

If you want to solicit the advice of someone you don't know, speak with someone who knows them or knows of them. Be articulate in your request and the motivation behind it. If an Old Money member of your community agrees to help you, you must respect their time and make the most of it.

* The Etiquette Institute of Washington, DC
* Dallas School of Etiquette

85

ETIQUETTE & MANNERS
That Was Then. This Is Now.

Manners. Politeness. Common courtesy. I can't emphasize these enough. At the risk of being redundant, please allow me to share some additional random thoughts on this important Core Value.

- Etiquette and manners consist of structured rituals, like saying, "Good morning," "Please," "Thank you," and "Excuse me," as well as spontaneous acts of kindness and generosity, such as holding a door open for someone else.

- Being polite makes it easier to move through the world and get things done.

- Being polite without being sincere is tricky business.

- Derogatory remarks about someone's sexuality are so 20th century.

- Talking "behind someone's back" is cheap and cowardly.

- The top level of conversation is the discussion of ideas or interests. The midrange is the discussion of current events. The low level is the discussion of other people, i.e., gossip. Take the high road.

• We all want to relax and enjoy ourselves in a social situation. That's easy to do if everyone knows the rules. Etiquette is the set of rules.

• The digital age has made communication obviously more fluid and, sadly, more casual. That, however, is no excuse for laziness. There are "best practices" that need to be mastered and "gold standards" that need to be preserved. Good behavior is a mark of civilization's progress. Let's honor the work of our ancestors.

• The digital age has made us impatient. We expect everything *now*. Information. Responses. Packages. Getting to know someone, however, takes time. This process is more enjoyable and productive when we're polite.

• Ironically, taking the time to be polite may expedite the process of getting information or results from another person, even in the most stressful and urgent situations.

• If you don't develop the habit of good manners and some of the technical proficiency in etiquette, you may pay a price at some point. Personally or professionally.

• If you can't be thoughtful and kind for a brief moment to a stranger on the subway, how are you going to be thoughtful and kind to your spouse every day over a lifetime?

• Courtesy is both a noble endeavor and a smart move.

• The world doesn't have time to coddle the unprepared. It doesn't have time to explain what should already be understood. It's looking for the whole package: the person who brings competence if not expertise, the ability and willingness to learn and adapt, and a polished, sincere manner when relating to others. Learn etiquette and manners now and be ready for opportunity whenever it presents itself.

• Know that manners are the unspoken access code of Old Money culture, a tell-tale signal that we look for when we consider bringing someone along or inviting someone in. That's a very transactional way of courtesy, but it's a reality nonetheless.

• I'd like you to be well-mannered because it's the right thing to do, not just the smart thing to do.

• If you're the boss, phrase your instructions like requests, even if they're not. "Could we get that meeting set today?"

• If you aspire to work or conduct business internationally, it is even more important for you to master a certain level of etiquette. Americans are generally very casual. The rest of the world is generally not.

• An essential part of being polite in another country is learning the language.

• When you're an American in another country, please remember that you're representing all of us.

• Being polite doesn't mean being phony. It means being your best self. Thinking of others first.

• Being polite doesn't mean being a doormat. It means conveying respect to others, gravitating to those who reciprocate, and ignoring those who don't.

• It's easy to be polite when others are polite. The challenge is to be polite when others are rude. This is the point at which etiquette and manners transform into breeding and refinement.

• The use of thank you notes has decreased significantly since I first published *The Old Money Book*. This is tragic. If you give someone a gift and they do not send a thank you note to acknowledge it, send them a box of thank you notes as their next gift. My wife won't let me do this, but you can do it.

• Society's need for etiquette and manners has only increased during this pandemic. People are stressed. Nerves are frayed. Tempers can flair. Remember that. Be even more polite.

• Socially distance, wear a mask, and wash your hands. One day we'll look back on all this and celebrate our triumph over it.

◊ ◊ ◊ ◊

As you learn the ins and outs of etiquette for dinner parties at home, business meetings on the road, and diplomatic functions abroad, you'll discover a single, simple concept behind it all. It's revealed below.

From *The Old Money Book* blog
Feb 24, 2020

Rules and Regs

I had a delightful conversation recently with a journalist who was interviewing me about my new book, *Old Money Style*.

I related what I was hoping to achieve with the book—the complete and total extinction of flip-flops, T-shirts, and cargo pants from the planet—and who the book was written for: young men graduating high school or college, and older men ready to upgrade their look.

Once we'd covered all of the fundamental points, the journalist confided in me that he'd attended boarding school (all boys, at the time). He understood intimately "the uniform" that I discuss in the book, both in theory and in practice. Then he shared a remarkable and memorable (for him and me) moment in his education.

He and his classmates arrived for their first term at school. Shortly thereafter, his entire freshman class was called to the main hall. They were to be informed of the "rules and regulations" that would inform and moderate their conduct as students. Expecting a monotonous litany of fatiguing "dos and don'ts," the freshman class shuffled in, plopped down in their seats, and readied themselves for a dusty rendition of what they could and could not do, what was obligatory and what was prohibited, what was expected and what was not tolerated. Ho hum.

The headmaster approached the podium, cleared his throat, and welcomed the class. He then said, "As for our rules and regulations that govern your behavior while you are a student at this institution, let me begin."

Exhales and rolling of the eyes commenced among the student body. The headmaster continued, "You are expected, at all times, to conduct yourselves as gentlemen." He then cast a firm eye over the assembly of young men. And left.

Initially baffled, then delighted, the freshman class looked at each other, shrugging and laughing off such a thin, vague edict. Then, a few of the freshman (I suspect the journalist I spoke to was among them) began to realize how restrictive the simple, straightforward commandment was: *they would have to conduct themselves*, it began...directing the governance of behavior to be the sole responsibility of the student, not the faculty. This, they soon realized, would put the burden of honorable, ethical, moral, and polite behavior squarely on them, collectively and individually.

Furthermore, there was no grace period and no recess. "*At all times*" was comprehensive, complete, all-encompassing, and immediate. They didn't get to ease into the concept at the start of their junior year. They didn't get to be gentlemen only during class, or only when someone was watching. And when they left campus for spring break or summer...? What then? No, "at all times" meant "*at all times.*"

And the term gentlemen...? Everybody knew what a gentleman was (and wasn't), and what gentlemanly behavior and conduct was (and wasn't), but why didn't the headmaster go into more detail? Provide some more definition? Clarify some term or quantify some boundary?

No, the genius of it lay in its conceptual and ephemeral nature: like the water that fish swim in and the wind that carries the birds across the sky, the concept of "being a gentleman at all times" would at once surround and support these unsuspecting freshmen. Moving easily within its currents would become second nature. Rising effortlessly upon its breeze would lift them, and carry them. It would be a constant, unseen, but essential part of their existence.

No fence or wall or threat of punishment could perform this function. Only a concept.

Not unlike "Old Money," I suppose.

FINANCIAL
INDEPENDENCE

*"There is no dignity quite so impressive, and no one independence
quite so important, as living within your means."*
— Calvin Coolidge

Financial independence is the fifth core value of Old
Money. After all, you can't be Old Money without
money. Saying that money does not buy happiness is missing
the point; the truth is you have more options when you have
money, and when you need money, there is rarely a substitute
for it.

When the general public thinks of wealthy people, they
think of them living in big houses, driving expensive cars, and
wearing fashionable clothes and flashy jewelry. Obviously,
some wealthy individuals and families do maintain a high
profile of conspicuous consumption and well-publicized
socializing.

Old Money response to such behavior: peacock today,
feather duster tomorrow. The priority for Old Money is financial independence, not display. If you have to get up in
the morning and go to a miserable job in order to pay for a
big house, expensive car, and high-end wardrobe, what's the

point? If you can get up each morning and do whatever you want to do that day—and every day—that's quite a luxury. Financial independence makes it easier to discover what it is you really enjoy doing, both regarding a vocation and regarding hobbies and leisure.

Financial independence is easier to maintain when you live simply and focus on *doing* and *being* more than *spending* and *having*. Old Money knows that material possessions can be cumbersome, so it chooses wisely. But don't think Old Money doesn't live well; it does. The convenience and comfort of quality clothing, a well-appointed home, a staff to take care of daily chores, private planes, and exotic travel—it's a good life. But it's not to be flaunted to those less fortunate, and it certainly is not an end unto itself.

Financial independence often requires hard work to acquire it and diligence to preserve it. That's why Old Money lives efficiently and quietly. Money not spent is money that can be saved and invested. More importantly, Old Money knows that buying things and spending money does not make one happy for any extended period of time. Old Money is fortunate, and it knows it. It does not squander, but it is not cheap, especially with family and friends. Old Money is an investor, not a consumer.

Old Money watches what it spends because, many times, Old Money is living on interest or dividend income from investments. This is usually a fixed monthly or quarterly amount generated by a substantial principal. The principal is rarely touched, as it is the goose that lays the golden eggs. Ideally, the goose will lay the golden eggs for this generation and the next. Therefore, Old Money becomes an expert at living within its means, and many times, well below its means. It seeks out value for each dollar spent. It spends slowly, almost always on quality. It knows that freedom means infinitely more than material possessions.

Perhaps most importantly, Old Money does not try to solve emotional or psychological problems by spending or giving money, or behaving extravagantly. Financial decisions are made logically and strategically, not emotionally.

Unlike most people, Old Money has made a budget and keeps it in mind when making decisions regarding expenditures. It has learned, from family most likely, the most efficient way to live. It knows what activities are truly enjoyable—work with purpose, life with passion, dinner with friends—and it makes the most of those.

There is a lot of joy, passion, and excitement living an Old Money kind of life. There just isn't much drama. Drama detracts from accomplishing things, enjoying life, and preserving financial independence.

The ability to gain and retain your financial independence amidst the onslaught of advertising, marketing, and promotion that is the modern world of commerce can be challenging. An infinite number of products and services—*New and improved! A real must-have this fall! For a limited time only!*—tempt us from an infinite number of sources (television, magazines, the internet). They promise a better life if only we will buy what they are selling. It can be difficult to resist.

In order to live within your means, you must know who you are. You must know what you like, what you don't like, what you want, and what you need, what works for you, regardless of what advertising tells you. You must have a strong sense of self, without being selfish or self-centered.

You must also know how much money you have (income and assets) and what responsibilities you have. You must have clear financial goals that are not related to accumulation of material possessions. You must have a life that is not related to or dependent upon consuming one retail product or service after another.

Once you've made the effort to get off of the consumer merry-go-round and focus on *doing and being* instead of *spending and having*, you will have a very strange epiphany: the constant passing parade of advertised products, services, sales, and alleged bargains will look strangely foreign. You will be fine without them. You will know that no single product is going to change your life, make you more popular, make you more productive, or make you a better person. You will be amused at those who boast about their new store-bought items, and a little sad for them as they invest so much of their self-esteem in the material things.

You will plan purchases, perhaps spending more for quality, but overall buying less, less often. You will spend much less time shopping, as you will go to a store to buy something you want or need, and leave. Shopping will be less of a social activity and more of a strategy: getting the highest quality product for your money, in the least amount of time, so you can get back to doing what you love. You will have more time and more money. You will wonder what you used to do that kept you so busy and, perhaps, so broke. You will be free.

Children and Money

Children learn financial habits and attitudes about money from their parents. The apple just doesn't fall far from the tree. Old Money knows that a generation without good financial habits is a generation—and possibly a fortune—lost.

When they're old enough, give your children a weekly allowance and teach them to budget their money. If they blow through their allowance before the week is out or don't have money for a special event, let them suffer. They'll be more attentive.

Encourage them to earn money by mowing lawns, babysitting, or starting a neighborhood or internet business.

Teach them to save over time in order to buy things they want in the future.

Teach them to shop wisely. If there's a new gadget that they absolutely must have, let them buy it with money they've earned. Over time, they will learn what has value and what doesn't.

Flamboyant displays of family wealth or boasting about family money are taboo. Children should know this.

Discussions about other people's money or possessions are off limits.

If your child breaks a rule, do not punish them by taking away their allowance. Money is not a tool to manipulate behavior. Punish your children by taking away privileges. They can have their allowance, but if they can't go hang out with their friends, money doesn't mean much. This is an important lesson: the role and limitations of money.

Passing It On

Old Money has prepared the next generation for handling wealth and privilege through example and education. It has also prepared for an orderly transition of the accumulated assets when one generation dies and the next inherits. *This limits the possibility of emotion overtaking logic during grief.* Even intelligent and well-intentioned people can do destructive, vindictive, and simply stupid things when they're upset over the loss of a loved one.

Therefore, no matter how young or how healthy it is, Old Money has a will prepared, signed, and notarized. You should, too. Simple and straightforward templates can be found online if your estate is small and heirs are limited in number. For larger estates, consult an attorney who specializes in this practice area.

Keep a copy of your will in a secure, fireproof place at home and a second copy with your attorney or in a safe deposit box. Make sure everyone in your family knows where the will is and knows that it accurately expresses your wishes. If your wishes change, change the will. Consider inserting a clause that will award one dollar to anyone who contests the will (ouch). This will discourage litigation among heirs, especially when the estate is substantial.

Consider carefully who you name as the executor of your will. Attorneys charge hourly rates for handling the dispensation of assets and are paid directly from the estate. If complications or litigation ensue, these fees can decimate an estate.

An emotional, inexperienced, or power-crazed executor, attorney or not, can wreak havoc on decades of hard work and careful planning. The executor should be made aware, prior to your death, that you want them to act in this capacity. They should be comfortable with this responsibility and have the time and ability to do it. You may consider videotaping the two of you reviewing your will verbally, on camera, to confirm the conditions set forth in it.

If you have young or irresponsible heirs who may need time to mature before receiving a substantial estate, consider holding the majority of an inheritance in a trust that cannot be accessed until they are older. Or give some now and the rest later. Real-world work and responsibilities over time will temper spending habits and forge a sense of identity separate and apart from inherited money.

Have clear instructions in your will or in a separate document (an Advanced Care Directive and/or a DNR) about what measures are to be followed if you are incapacitated and/or on life support in a hospital. The names of these documents may differ state by state. Ask your physician, attorney, or local hospital for the appropriate forms and with whom they need to be filed. Medical expenses for long-term care can add to the already considerable grief your family will experience. Address this difficult subject in writing. Make sure your doctor and family have a copy and that everyone knows your wishes.

Limit the funeral expenses. You are loved and will be remembered, but not fondly, if the costs of your memorial service consume half the inheritance.

If you're older and set for life, consider giving some money to your heirs while you're alive, but keep enough for yourself. You don't want to outlive your money.

Helpful Hints

- It's not how much you make. It's how you manage what you make.

• Write down your financial goals. Look at them every two months. Assess your progress. Adjust accordingly.

• Know why you're working, planning, saving, and investing.

• Do not buy things to fill emotional needs. Work, religion, family, and friends fill emotional needs.

• When you see something in a store, ask yourself: "What will happen if I don't buy this?" If it's food and you don't want to be hungry, buy it. If it's optional and you'll honestly feel no different, don't buy it. If you'd feel like you missed out on a real value—*and you can afford it*—consider it. And if you do buy it, pay cash.

• The first things you buy are the things you use every day. Then you purchase things you use every week. Then things you use seasonally. If you are only using something once a year, give serious thought as to why you are buying it.

• Don't shop when you're really upset or really ecstatic. Shop on an even keel.

• When shopping is a social activity and done with friends, remember that you don't have to buy anything. It's about friendship, not spending.

• Do not feel peer pressure to buy an expensive gift for someone if you cannot afford it. If someone gives you an expensive gift, thank them. If they expect you to reciprocate in kind, feel free to let them be disappointed.

- Buy gifts and give them for the joy of giving, not as a social obligation. Always remember birthdays and other important dates, but always give within your means. This will prevent resentment.

- Put more thought into a gift and you will often spend less money on it.

- If you can't spend a lot of money on a gift, take the person out for a coffee or a drink. Spend time with them. Tell them what they mean to you. To hear that can be quite a present.

- There are get-rich-quick schemes and get-rich-quick screams. One is from those who fall for the other.

- Look at items in your home or closet that have not been used in 12 months. Ask yourself why you bought them. Remember how you answer. Pack them up and give them away to someone who can use them.

- If you give them to charity, get a receipt and write it off your taxes.

- When you get a promotion, pay increase, or windfall, reward yourself and those you care for with a small percentage of it. Make sure your reward has lasting value: something of quality, something with meaning. Take pride. Feel good. Celebrate. But be circumspect about how much you share—money and information—with others. Put the rest of the money away.

- Financial or investment advice you see on television or read in a magazine, newspaper, or online is usually substandard. Solid investment advice is most consistently communicated person-to-person, face-to-face, by a professional who has spent many years working and learning how the financial markets function and how various investment products perform. These advisors can be very good at their job and have a great track record, but remember, they're giving you their *best guess*, and that's all. Do your own homework.

• Nobody will look after your money like you.

• Ask the investment advisor if they're invested in the same products they're recommending to you.

• Do not take investment advice from poor people, for obvious reasons.

• Every investment has risk.

• Know your comfort level for risk.

• Know that you must risk in order to make progress, in life or in investments.

• Manage your risks.

• Learn something from every mistake. Remember what you learned. Never make the same mistake twice.

• Avoid big mistakes.

• Before you invest a dime, think about how long it's taken for you to accumulate the money you're considering investing. If you inherited it, think of how long it took your ancestors to accumulate it.

• It is an obvious truth that a stockbroker believes that stocks are a good investment.

• Ask for references from anyone who wants to handle or invest your money. Do research. Call those references and, if possible, meet them in person.

• Moderate your personal involvement with those who handle your money. You may have to fire them.

• Regardless of the economic climate, there are always investments performing well.

• Extravagance is the fear of poverty and the need for attention. Discretion is the fear of nothing and the need of nothing.

• The only acceptable display of wealth is charity. If you want to have the wing of the children's hospital named after you, go for it.

• Keep a journal; write down what you spend money on every day at the very moment you spend it. Do this for 30 days. You will eliminate wasteful habits.

• Work hard. Live below your means. Save and invest your money wisely. When you can afford a luxury, acquire it and enjoy it unapologetically (but best in private).

• Do not be cheap with your family and friends. Do not be foolish, either.

• Earn steadily. Save regularly. Spend slowly.

• Carefully review your monthly expenses. Consider alternatives. What if you didn't pay a hundred dollars a month or more for cable television? What if you didn't pay retail for weekly manicures and pedicures?

• Give to a reputable charity, regardless of your income level.

• Most of the really enjoyable things in life don't require a large capital outlay. Find those. Do those.

• Do not use credit cards, debit cards, or ATM cards to buy things. Pay cash. You will spend less and have more.

• Do not discuss your financial situation with friends. Discuss your financial situation with family selectively.

• Keep your assets highly liquid, the return on investment steady, and your overhead low. Do the math: if you lost your job tomorrow, could you live for 3 months on the money you have in the bank? Could you live 6 months? A year? Could you live comfortably on investment income for 5 years? The rest of your life? Are your children taken care of? Your grandchildren? Forget expensive cars and gauche jewelry. This is the Old Money measure of wealth.

• There is a reason Old Money spends money the way it does on the things it does and prepares the way it does. Think about it. Analyze it. Imitate it. Benefit from it.

For Reference

The Millionaire Next Door by Thomas J. Stanley and William D. Danko offers surprising insights into the thinking, spending habits, and lifestyles of American millionaires.

The Relationship

A highly qualified certified public accountant (CPA) is critical to financial well-being. You don't want to get into trouble with the IRS, but you don't want to pay any more taxes than you have to. As your wealth grows, this person or firm will become even more important.

The CPA may recommend you to a money manager. If they do, ask the CPA if this person handles his or her personal portfolio. Ask them how well their investments have performed. Ask the CPA if they have clients that you could speak with who also use this investment advisor. When you speak with these clients, ask them how long they've been with this investment advisor or firm. How did they come to be a client with the investment advisor? How have their investments performed over the long term? Do they have any complaints about the services provided? Ask. Ask. Ask.

An experienced and successful investment advisor will be valuable as you adopt the suggestions in this book and begin to consider what to do with your surplus cash. Money management is a profession, not a hobby or sideline. You should not be the manager's only client. You should not be their wealthiest client. This person or firm should assess your risk tolerance and goals and give you investment options to choose from.

They should not pressure you into investments or decisions. If you can find an investment advisor who works with Old Money families in your area, talk to him. There may be minimum portfolio requirements ($1 million is not uncommon), but there may also be the opportunity to develop a relationship. So don't be intimidated or put off.

FINANCIAL
INDEPENDENCE
That Was Then. This Is Now.

The coronavirus outbreak and subsequent economic fallout has left many people unemployed, financially drained, and very afraid.

Flowery talk about "living your dreams" is not something you need if you are facing a challenging moment with your personal finances because of COVID-19.

So I'm going to give you, first, some working definitions of possible sources of income and second, some ways to measure "financial independence." These will help you get a mental handle on where you are and where you want to go.

I'm also going to present some very fundamental, nuts-and-bolts strategies and suggestions that can help get you and your family through this storm, to the other side.

First, it would be wise to itemize and define the eight primary categories of income and some common sources for each. This may help you discover untapped sources of income that you have access to, possibilities that you can develop and exploit in the future. Remember: it's best to have more than one source of income because you can make more each month, obviously. You're also in a better position to survive and adapt if you lose a source of income and still have another source of income available.

Here we go:

- **Earned Income** - this is income you earn from getting a paycheck, going to work each week as an employee. The advantage to having this type of income is the relative security and predictability it offers. You know how many hours you have to work, what you have to do, and what you will be paid. A job may also offer benefits like paid vacation, medical insurance, stock options, or profit sharing. The disadvantage to this type of income is that it may not be sufficient to meet your monthly needs or lifetime goals. You may also be laid off at any time.

- **Profit Income** - this is income that comes from purchasing goods at a wholesale price and selling them at a retail price, or from offering services like towing cars or painting houses, that customers pay you to perform. Business owners, professional investors, skilled craftsmen, lawyers, and doctors enjoy profit income when the revenues from their work exceed expenses. The advantage of this type of income is that there is sometimes no limit to how much money you can make. The disadvantage is that you may also lose money, especially if markets change or if you become sick or injured.

- **Interest Income** - this income usually comes when you deposit your money in a financial institution and that bank or credit union pays you interest for the privilege of using it. The advantage to this is that your money is probably safe and growing, but the disadvantage is that the interest rate may be very small when compared to other investments you could make.

• **Rental Income** - if you own a building, house, or piece of land, you have the option to rent the apartments, offices, buildings, or land to others to live in, work in, or raise animals on. The advantages to this income stream are that you may have a reliable source of income for a long time with good tenants. The disadvantages to owning rental property are that you may not be able to rent it or rent it profitably if the demand for your property decreases. You may also have tenants who are unable or unwilling to pay rent. And there's always the chance that natural disasters can damage your property, impacting your rental income.

• **Dividend Income** - this is income earned from investments in stocks or other financial instruments that pay monthly or quarterly dividends to you for the privilege of using your money. It is by far the most popular form of income for Old Money families. The advantages are that companies offering dividends usually pay a higher rate of interest than banks, and that solid, well-managed companies or funds can be reliable in the long term. Some dividends can be tax free (municipal bonds, for example). The disadvantages are that, like all businesses, companies or funds paying dividends are vulnerable to market fluctuations (pandemics, recessions, etc.), which may impact their ability to pay dividends at a consistent rate in the future.

• **Capital Gains Income** - this income results from the one-time sale of an asset—real estate or stocks, usually—at a sale price that is greater than the acquisition price. In other words, you sold it for more than you paid for it. Let's say you purchased 100 shares of a stock, and the per share price increased. You have the option to sell some or all of the shares and make a profit. In this scenario, there is no limit to how much a stock or piece of real estate might be worth when markets change. That's a great advantage. The disadvantages to this income stream are that it is usually highly taxed, and it only happens once with a single asset in a single transaction.

• **Residual Income** - this income originates from work that has been previously performed. Actors, for example, often receive residuals for commercials, television series, or movies in which they appeared. The advantages to this income are that it requires no effort on your part to receive and may be paid to you forever. The disadvantages are that its amount and frequency are dependent upon market forces (popularity of a television series over time, for example), and you usually have no control over those forces.

• **Royalty Income** - this income is usually the result of intellectual properties being licensed or exploited by third parties in the marketplace. These intellectual properties may be patents on inventions, trademarks for iconic brands, rights to motion pictures and television series, photographs, popular songs, or even the rights to a famous person's name or likeness. The advantages of this income stream are similar to those of residual income in that the revenue may come in over a long period of time and only require proper management to be very profitable. And, again, the disadvantages are that this income is vulnerable to the marketplace's ever-changing tastes.

If you're like many people right now, you may simply be trying to maintain the primary income source you have (your job) and get through the worst of this economic crisis without going into debt or using up all of your savings. If you have the advantage of a well-paying or at least secure job, you may have the chance to set aside cash. If you can stack up the cash to cover six months' worth of living expenses, great. Work toward that as quickly as possible.

If you already have six months' living expenses in cash, then you have the opportunity to investigate acquiring or developing income-producing assets. An asset, remember, can be defined as something that puts money in your pocket every month. Most of the income sources I described above generate their income from assets.

What affluent people do that many other people do not do is this: they take part of the income they receive from one source, let's say a job or profession, and purchase an asset with it. This asset then produces a second income stream. Let's say, for example, the asset acquired is a stock that pays dividends. That dividend income is then used to purchase another asset, let's say a rental property. And so on. This is called stacking your assets.

Of course, affluent people have the initial funds to do this, you say. True, but sometimes they simply begin this process by not purchasing consumer products such as big-screen televisions or brand-new cars. Instead, they take that money and invest in something that's going to provide income to them, and may increase in value over time, as well.

This opportunity to acquire assets and build wealth over time is available to most people. It simply requires awareness (the difference in how you're using money), education (learning about different assets and how they work), and discipline (consistently investing in assets that produce income streams, rather than purchasing consumer products that do nothing).

It's critical to not waste money. It's also critical to not waste time. You can make different choices today with the money and time you have right now. I hope you'll make wise choices.

Now, where will these different choices lead you?

Good choices over time will probably lead you to what is often referred to as "financial independence." So let's get a clearer picture of this frequently used concept by breaking the term down into three levels:

- a minimum level of financial independence;

- an intermediate level of financial independence; and

- an optimum level of financial independence.

If someone has a minimum level of financial independence, they have a small amount of savings, or perhaps none. They need to have a job or a reliable source of income that generates money every week. If they become unemployed or their source of income stops, it is likely that they will need to find another job or another source of income almost immediately to avoid financial trouble. People at this level have about two weeks to a month of financial independence. If there are health issues within the family, their financial situation is at even greater risk.

A person at an intermediate level of financial independence could lose their job or their source of income and be okay for a couple of months, or even a couple of years. They could dip into savings and/or live off of some investment income, but they would eventually need to go back to work or create another source of income in order to maintain their standard of living and preserve their financial security. If they didn't go back to work at some point, they might be forced to liquidate assets or reduce their standard of living severely in order to survive.

When people discuss "financial independence" today, they are most likely referring to optimum financial indepen-

109

dence. At this level of financial independence, a person can lose or quit their job, or lose their primary source of income, and live for the rest of their lives without worry, without lowering their standard of living, and without any impact on future plans they have for themselves or their families.

This is the position that Old Money families and individuals are in. While many have large amounts of cash on hand, most live off the income from rental property, dividends from stocks and bonds, annuities, intellectual property royalties, or any number of other sources that generate what is often referred to as "passive income." It is "passive" because it requires no effort or work to receive.

Understanding these levels of financial independence is important. It can give you a clearer picture of where you want to go and how to get there. However, it's imperative to understand where you are right now and how to address your current situation, especially if times are tough. So let's get to that.

During difficult times, life becomes math. Your main focus becomes increasing your monthly income and reducing your monthly expenses. The government will, hopefully, provide some assistance and relief to working families, but, until then, it's up to each and every one of us to take stock of how much money we have coming in, where it's going, and how we can have more money left over at the end of each month.

It's that simple. I will say this: it is much easier for people to deal with financial stress if they set aside "what other people might think" and "things I just have to have" prior to making choices and executing plans. In the first instance, "other people" probably aren't thinking of anyone but themselves right now. In the second instance, what human beings really "need" is not a double mocha decaf latte, but food, shelter, and clothing. Most items after food, shelter, and clothing are luxuries, and a lot of luxuries get put on hold during a financial crisis. And make no mistake, we are in one right now.

So let's talk first about increasing your income. If you are unemployed or in need of cash, the easiest thing to do is to look around and see what you can quickly and conveniently sell for cash. This may be something as large as your home or something as small as your television. You may soon be hosting a garage sale or an open house, depending on your situation. But if that's what you need to do, consider doing it. Make smart decisions. Do not sell a car that you may need to get to and from work, but feel free to sell that exercise equipment that's just sitting in the spare bedroom.

The second way to bring in more income is to work longer hours or find a second job. This seems obvious, but it doesn't occur to a lot of people. What's more, when you're working, you're not spending. You're earning. So your expenses will likely decrease at the same time.

Also note that teenagers are not exempt from working and contributing to the household income. This is a team effort, with the goal being to get the family out of this temporary situation and back to a certain financial level. After-school jobs may be part of the plan. Cleaning houses, catering, babysitting or becoming an Uber driver are unglamorous but viable options. The "gig economy" is real.

Companies like Upwork, Fiverr, and PeoplePerHour offer freelancers the opportunity to promote their services and skills, interact with companies and individuals who are hiring, and get paid. Investigate these sites and others and see what skill set you might have that can generate extra income.

It's also good to remember that even during the worst economic times, wealthy people are still spending money. They still need goods and services, and most are willing to pay a fair price to get them. If you need to earn money, or more money, consider reaching out to business owners or entrepreneurs in your community and expressing an interest in working for them or with them. Have some idea as to what you can do and do well, or what you want to do in the future. (Tutor their children, manage their real estate...) Explain as much as you think necessary about why you're looking for work. Don't try to play on their emotions. Just develop a plan, rehearse a short script, and take the initiative with a phone call or an email. If they do respond and offer you an opportunity, do your best, work hard, and honor their generosity. If they decline, thank them sincerely and move on without resentment.

Starting an online or home-based business may be something to consider during this time. Remember to objectively analyze opportunities and base your decisions on real numbers, not pie-in-the-sky promises from YouTube "millionaires." A lot of people claim to be millionaires on YouTube, just like they claim to be on Instagram. Know that a profitable business requires having a solid plan and hard work. It's founded on providing goods and services with value to paying customers. Again, it's that simple.

The government is always hiring, whether it's at a local, state, or federal level. Look for work there.

If you have some time and some money, look for a certification that can (cost-effectively) give you more value in the job market, or in a particular profession.

The second part of the equation is cutting expenses. As I mentioned, if you own a home or a piece of real estate and you need money, consider putting your home up for sale or renting it out and renting a smaller, less expensive place for yourself. If you are renting and need to not have that expense, consider asking a family member or close friend if you can stay with them for a period of time until you get back on your feet.

Yes, this may be a humbling experience. It can also be an enriching experience when you discover firsthand how kind and generous people can be. Again, come up with a plan and take the initiative. Know what you plan to do with the money you're going to save by not paying retail for rent. (Offering your host money for utilities and the inconvenience would be a classy thing to do.) Know how long you'll need to get back on your feet. Have an idea of where you're going to go when you are back on your feet.

If you think that you may be homeless in a matter of weeks or months, go online now and locate all of the local food and shelter resources available in your area. Churches, nonprofits, and municipalities are dealing with these economic ramifications every day and may be able to help. Communicate with your creditors and your landlord. Everyone knows the situation. Some people may work with you to postpone or forgive obligations. Just ask.

If you just need to make the money you earn go farther, it's time to look at smaller expenses. A simple place you can start is with your grocery bill. By pivoting on this front, you can save money and eat healthier by adopting a plant-based diet.

This means eliminating beef, chicken, pork, fish, and lamb from your grocery list. If you are really serious about cutting down on the food bill, locate the Indian market in your area. They sell five- and ten-pound bags of rice and dried beans. Options include garbanzo beans, red beans, black beans, lima beans, and black-eyed peas, as well as basmati rice, brown rice, and jasmine rice, to name but a few.

Indian markets also sell sauces, spices, and herbs to give your rice and beans a wonderful variety of flavors. If you supplement this go-to dish with fresh vegetables like cabbage, broccoli, potatoes, eggplant, cauliflower, zucchini, and green peas or green beans, you'll find a new way to get the nutrition you need without the expense of processed foods.

With a bottle of olive oil, two pots, and a stove, you can refine your eating habits and survive on very little money for a very long time if necessary. Leaning in this direction (a vegetarian or vegan diet) will cut your food costs immediately and probably keep you healthier in the long run (reducing the likelihood of medical bills, prescription medications, and over-the-counter medicines as well). If you search for *vegan or vegetarian recipes* on the internet, you find plenty of nutritious, delicious, and economical meal options.

Avoiding fast food is a given. Paying retail for alcohol and food at bars and restaurants is probably not in the cards for awhile if you're trying to budget and cut costs.

Birthday presents for the kids are best if they are cash or books. Family and friends can be gently advised of the shift in priorities and asked to contribute to your daughter's college fund rather than contributing to the quarterly profits of a toy or clothing manufacturer. Again, take a clue from our Indian brothers and sisters: they start giving children gold and gold jewelry at a very young age, and continue that practice into adulthood. Toys get put in the closet or thrown away. Gold appreciates.

If you need to purchase clothes, make sure the garments you need to buy are going to help you make money, i.e., for a job interview or for work. Your purchases are for things you will wear every day, not special occasions. Ladies, consult *Old Money, New Woman* for suggestions on what to buy, where to buy it, and how to wear it. Gents, check out *Old Money Style* and invest in what I call "The Uniform."

"The Uniform" is, very briefly, a navy blazer, an oxford cloth button down shirt, khakis or grey slacks, and brown shoes, with a striped necktie. This ensemble will serve you well for a multitude of social events and is appropriate for a wide variety of occupations and workplaces.

During this time, credit cards are best used to purchase gasoline for your car and food for your kitchen only, and only if you can't pay cash. Everything else is paid for with cash or put on hold. Credit card interest is a savage beast, and it can't be written off on your income taxes.

Quality time spent with friends and family is key. We all need the emotional support, and we all need to be reminded of what's really important, especially now. For the most part, we are a nation of immigrants. We encourage those who have a dream and empathize with those who face challenges. Few of us are so self-reliant that we don't need the goodwill of others. Many of us can afford to help out a friend or neighbor in need. This is the time to remember these truths and act accordingly.

My thoughts and prayers are with each of you during this time. I hope some of the suggestions presented here can help and offer at least some sense of comfort and direction.

◊ ◊ ◊ ◊

In this chapter on financial independence, I've focused much of my message on how to make the best use of your money. This blog post offers insight on making the best use of another precious resource. Enjoy.

From *The Old Money Book* blog
January 19, 2019

The Sentry

Once upon a time, a prince was asked to explain how he came to be so wise. As members of his court fell silent and attentive, the prince thought for a moment, and then shared this story:

"I was very undisciplined as a child, easily distracted and soft of character. My father saw this, and when I turned 16, he sent me on a journey through the country. I was to travel to the next kingdom and introduce myself to the sovereign there. It was to be my first diplomatic mission, and I was very excited, and very full of myself.

"I expected to travel by carriage with a retinue of attendants and trunks full of clothes, furs, food and wine. But when I stepped into the courtyard of the palace to depart, a lone sentry stood there with two horses. I would travel with only a sword, a change of clothes, and money for food and simple accommodations along the way. Such were the orders of my father. Because he was king, no one would listen to me, and I had no choice but to travel with only my cloak and hat to protect me from the elements.

"So the sentry, who said little during our journey, was my only companion. The first two days, everything was fine. The weather was pleasant and the accommodations and food acceptable. I slept in a simple room, and the sentry nodded outside my locked door as a precaution. On the third day, the rain came down upon us not an hour into our journey. I turned to the sentry and said, 'Let's go back to the village and wait for the rain to stop.'

" 'No,' he said, 'You cannot go back.'

"Who was he to speak to me like this? I turned my horse, and he pulled his sword.

" 'I have my orders,' he said quite seriously. I had no doubt he was telling the truth. If he was not, when we returned to my family's palace and I told my father he had been untruthful about an order from the king, he would be put to death.

"So on we went through the rain. The next day, the weather turned cold. I forgot my scarf at the inn, but the sentry would not allow me to return for it. I was cold and angry, but on we went. One night, I had too much to drink at a tavern. I thought I was fine the next morning, but two hours into our day's ride, I felt sick, but I could not go back and rest. At a village in the country, I met a girl. In a single day, I fell in love and was certain she loved me. But the next day, we had to leave, and, of course, I could not go back. On another day, we encountered merchants with fine rugs and gold jewelry. I could not buy them, though, because I was on a mission and could not carry such a load of unnecessary things.

"As each day passed, I woke up knowing that I had to remember all of my belongings. I had to be attentive to what I ate and drank. I had to be kind to the people I met because if I said something hurtful, I could not go back to apologize or explain. If I felt something for someone, I had to tell them then and there, because I could not go back and express my feelings later. I could not acquire unnecessary things. I had to focus on my journey and prepare myself to meet the sovereign.

"Finally, after 10 days on the road, my sentry and I entered the gates of the sovereign's city. By this time I was not easily distracted. I was not soft. I was moderate in my appetites and steady in my saddle. My words had become my promises. The present had become my domain. I knew that the route back to my father's kingdom might not be the same, and that the people I had met on my journey I might never see again.

"As we dismounted at the front door, the sovereign's soldiers took the reins of our horses. The sentry and I walked through the massive series of doors and down a long hallway. Through a final set of doors we slowly walked, and the sovereign stood to greet us.

" 'Welcome,' he said. 'How was your journey?'

" 'Enlightening,' I said. 'I learned much and hope that I can be of service to you. My father sends his best wishes.'

"The sovereign smiled warmly and reciprocated his goodwill. 'May I show you to your chambers? We can dine and talk this evening.'

" 'Thank you,' I said. 'My sentry will—'

"As I turned to my sentry, I noticed for the first time that he was not there. 'My sentry...'

" '...is gone,' said the sovereign, completing my thought. 'You will never see him again.'

" 'I don't understand,' I said, now suddenly afraid, in a stranger's palace, unarmed and unprotected.

" 'Fear not,' said the sovereign. 'His mission is done. He provided the same service for your father, and for me, and for many now wise and enlightened men.'

" 'I still don't understand,' I said.

" 'That was not a man who came with you. That was Time. I trust you learned your lessons well from him.'

"And so, dumbfounded for a moment, I realized I had learned my lessons. And, if I am wise at all, that is how I came to be."

FAMILY & MARRIAGE

"A happy family is but an earlier heaven."
— *George Bernard Shaw*

The success of the marriage and the success of the family unit is the sixth core value of Old Money, but it may be the single most important one. Divorce, domestic violence, drug and alcohol abuse, unplanned pregnancies, spoiled or maladjusted children—these are deadly to Old Money, or money of any age.

Nobody knows what's going to happen when they get married. But there are things Old Money does to tilt the odds of happiness and success in their favor. Consider these as you contemplate marriage and family.

Old Money marries later in life and marries once. Chemistry is important, but shared values are more important. Chemistry will come and go, but shared values (like the ones documented in this book), where a couple is going, and what behavior is acceptable—those keep people together. Old Money couples have a very clear idea about what their lives and future are supposed to be like. Not because their parents had money and they have money, but because their parents had a common set of values and they have a common set of values. They also have clear expectations about their lives together. Things change as life goes on, but these shared values and expectations remain and keep couples on the same track.

Old Money is never in a rush to get married. You shouldn't be, either. If you truly believe your love is eternal, why not date for a while? A three-year engagement is good. It gives you time to see how the other person reacts to life's ups and downs. It gives you time to go through things as a couple. People can change in unexpected ways. A long engagement gives you both the opportunity to experience these changes, assess them, and adjust to them. And feel free not to announce your engagement to the world. It takes the social pressure off making a decision to end the relationship if things don't go according to plan. While you're engaged, you can simply say to friends and family, "We're dating each other exclusively right now."

Get feedback. It's not just in the movies: when a single Old Money person begins to get even remotely serious about a potential mate, the potential mate is scrutinized intensely by Old Money friends and the Old Money family. Suspicion or disapproval usually ends things quickly. Once you start dating someone who may be a potential mate, you should introduce them to your friends and family, too. If your friends and family do not like the prospective spouse, that may be a signal that something is amiss, either with them or the potential spouse. Have the courage to ask (in private) candid questions about any misgivings they might have about the person you are dating. Do not react to their responses, which may be painful to hear. Listen. Digest. Then consider your options and your way forward. It is often said that you don't just marry your spouse; you marry the family. Keep that in mind.

Gents, be smart about the ring. If you are under the illusion, perpetrated by the diamond industry, that you should spend three times your monthly salary on your bride's engagement or wedding ring, snap out of it. It's not a contest; it's a relationship. It's also the first major financial decision you're going to make as you start your life together. Don't blow it by paying retail for a piece of jewelry. If your chosen one requires a ring that she knows is beyond your means, weigh that. Consumers never have enough, and there may be self-esteem issues she (or you) needs to address.

Ladies, if you absolutely must have something large and sparkling to show your girlfriends and the world, snap out of it. It's the start of a life together, not a fairy tale. If your chosen one feels like he has to buy you an expensive ring even if he can't afford it, weigh that. Being financially responsible is a habit, and it takes two to make a successful marriage.

Everybody, be smart about the wedding. At the time of this writing, the average wedding in America costs $30,000. This spending, by mostly the middle class, occurs during a time when consumer debt, student loans, unemployment, and recession run rampant. Old Money is bewildered at this kind of behavior.

Consider saving the money that would have been spent on a lavish wedding. Use it wisely for the benefit of the new-lyweds and their children. Student loans can be eliminated or greatly reduced. Conservative investments can be made to form the initial nest egg for a young couple, reducing the stress of potential unemployment or making it possible for them to pursue a passion while underemployed (is the bride or groom an artist or musician?). Money can be set aside for continuing education to boost the bride or groom's career and income-earning potential in the future (could the bride or groom benefit from having an MBA?). If both the bride and groom are educated, on solid financial ground, and happy with their careers, a trust fund can be set up for the education of their children who haven't even been born yet.

Have candid conversations about the wedding partic-ulars and financial priorities with the future in-laws. If you or anyone in your family believe there absolutely must be a lavish, talk-of-the-town, fairy-tale wedding in order to fulfill some fantasy and make someone's life complete, ask why. Is this about the bride and groom, or some perceived position in the community? Whom do you wish to impress? At what price? Newlyweds, do you want a lavish wedding? Or do you want a life together? A wedding lasts a day, or three, in some cultures. A life together by definition lasts a lifetime, and how a young couple starts their lives together can make a world of difference.

Old Money is prepared, emotionally and financially, to make a commitment. You should be, too. You should think it through. Emotions are powerful. So is rent. Numerous honest and articulate discussions about making a life together never hurt any couple. If the passion cools considerably in the hard light of day, weigh that. If thinking and planning a future together reasonably and thoughtfully only ignites more passion, you may have chosen the right mate.

With all due respect to everyone's religious beliefs, use birth control. Nothing strains a relationship or sidetracks a couple's progress like an unexpected pregnancy, married or not. Pregnancy changes everything, and the younger and less established a couple is, the more drastic the changes will be. Finances are the most obvious source of strain, but an unplanned pregnancy can put hopes, dreams, education, and careers on the back burner, or out of reach altogether. This can foster resentment, unhappiness, and ultimately a separation or divorce. Plan.

If you are just starting out, have children later in life. Ask yourself, who is more prepared to be a parent: an 18-year-old or a 28-year-old?

Have fewer children, or don't have any at all. The planet is a finite place, and the world population is growing at an incredible rate. Closer to home, if you and your partner are struggling to care for one child, don't have another. It's that simple. Nothing keeps families in poverty like continuous pregnancies that a family has not planned for. And if you don't have any children, the world will not come to an end.

Old Money families have clear boundaries. For you, this means keeping extended family in their place. Well-intentioned relatives can come on strong when a couple first gets married or has their first child. Be grateful for their love and support, but draw the line with meddling. Be polite

121

when you communicate the boundaries to relatives, but be firm. You and your partner and your child are the immediate family unit now, as well as a part of a bigger family unit. Make your own rules and solve your own problems. Go to relatives for help and advice only as a last resort. Anything unflattering that you tell your parents about your spouse will be held against them (the spouse) for a very long time, perhaps forever. Even after the difficult time has passed, and you've returned to marital bliss, your parents will remember what you told them. So don't tell them anything but good things.

An Example

Jack, who aspires to be Old Money, has just graduated from college. He is in his early twenties. He has student loans to pay off. While still living at home with his parents, he finds a job. It does not pay as well as he'd hoped, but there is opportunity for advancement, and that's what he's looking for. Instead of immediately going out, renting an apartment and racking up a host of monthly living expenses, Jack sits down with his parents and has a heart-to-heart conversation.

He tells them that he wants to remain at home for the next year or two. His reasons are twofold: he wants to pay down his student loan, as well as save money. He's done a budget, and he shares it with them. He offers his parents a fair amount of money to cover his food and utilities while he lives at home; he itemizes how much he's going to pay on his student loan each month; he itemizes how much he's going to put in the bank each month *and not take out for any reason*; and he also mentions that he plans on taking one weekend per month and going out of town (or at least out of the house) to give them a respite.

His parents, impressed by his forethought, agree. They ask only that he pay for his groceries and not play the drums after 10 pm (wink, nod). They also agree to certain house rules—Jack's an adult, but it's their home—and they'll communicate often and honestly on a regular basis about how the living arrangement is working.

Eighteen months later, Jack has reduced his student loan debt substantially. He has also managed to accumulate a very nice cash nest egg for his future. He did not use credit cards; he stayed under budget; he did not have to pay rent.

And, oh yes, Jack got a promotion at work. Now, he has options. He can double down on his student loan payments; he can move into a one bedroom apartment and still save money and pay off his debt; or he can decide to live at home another six months, and really, really save money.

During this time, Jack has met Jill. Jill is also living with her parents and starting her career as an artist. Her income is not as steady or as substantial as Jack's, but her potential as an artist is strong. It's also what she loves to do. Her uncle is an Old Money Guy (OMG), and she learned about money and work from him.

Jack and Jill agree on a three-year engagement. This will give Jack time to improve his position financially, and it will also give Jill time to pursue her career as an artist. They will not get pregnant. They will not purchase a ridiculous engagement ring to impress anyone (I don't repeat things because *I'm* forgetful, I repeat things because *you're* forgetful). They will reduce their respective debt and save as much as they can. They will enjoy life. They will be in love.

By the time they marry, Jack will have been promoted again. His student loan debt may be paid off. He will have a very, very nice nest egg. Jill's art will be selling and generating income, in addition to her day job. They will have their modest wedding in her uncle's back yard. It's big enough (wink, nod). They will leave on their honeymoon more financially sound than many of their peers, and they will not yet be 30 years old.

Many readers might scoff at this scenario as unrealistic, but Italians, Indians, and Iranians have been doing it for generations, with admirable results.

Helpful Hints

• Look at her mother: that's how she's going to look in 30 years.

• Look at how he treats his siblings: that's how he's going to treat you in 3 years.

• If you would not consider marrying someone, do not date them.

• Do not rely on luck or promises to avoid pregnancy or disease. Use a condom.

• If you, your future spouse, or your family is not rich, keep the wedding simple and inexpensive.

• If you have doubts about the marriage immediately before the ceremony, do not marry.

• If you can't afford to be married, do not marry.

• When you marry, it's a partnership.

• Continue dating after you marry. Look nice. Send flowers. Light candles.

• Do not discuss your spouse's faults with others. This makes you look stupid for marrying them.

• Do not discuss your sex life with anyone but your partner or a professional therapist.

• When you consider infidelity, you are not playing with fire. You are playing with dynamite.

• Avoid ultimatums.

• Laugh.

For Reference

1001 Questions to Ask Before You Get Married by Monica Mendez Leahy is a fun and revealing source for couples about to embark upon the Big Adventure.

The Relationship

The most important one: the one with your spouse.

FAMILY & MARRIAGE
That Was Then. This Is Now.

As I've mentioned, after writing *The Old Money Book*, I was asked by many readers to write a book on dating, relationships, and marriage. So I did. It is entitled *The Old Money Guide To Marriage - Getting It Right, Making It Last.* It's partially based on tried-and-true traditions, strategies, and philosophy that Old Money has developed and practiced over the years in order to do the following:

- preserve their quality of life;

- preserve their wealth; and most importantly,

- raise healthy, happy, and productive children.

It's also based on my experiences: I have been happily married to the same woman for over 30 years, so I may have some idea of what works and what doesn't.

I'd encourage anyone who is dating, getting serious, or getting married to pick up a copy of the book—actually two copies: one for you, one for your partner—and read it carefully.

If you are the parent of a teenager, purchase a copy and leave it lying around the house. Eventually, your child will pick it up out of curiosity and hopefully absorb some of what

I've written. Or you could make it required reading prior to them going on their first date.

The pandemic has absolutely no effect on marriage. It is still wonderful. It is still work.

Below is an excerpt from *The Old Money Guide To Marriage* that addresses the stages of life that many of us go through as individuals and as couples. In looking at life from this perspective, the decisions we make about relationships—and when we make them—may improve. And that's a good thing, both for us and the ones we love.

The Stages of Life

The human species and its social structure have evolved over centuries. Today, in much of the developed world for many people, there are predictable stages of life that we can all recognize. Understanding these phases can provide a perspective about why, how, and when marriage fits into the grand scheme of things.

First, obviously, you're born. (Wink, nod.) In infancy, childhood, adolescence, and even young adulthood you may be completely dependent upon your parents or family structure for your physical needs, as well as your emotional needs. You are a student, most likely, attending school, but also learning about the world around you and how it functions. Your concerns seem large to you, but are really small. Your parents or older family members share the biggest responsibilities for making sure you're safe, fed, and cared for.

In young adulthood, you begin to make decisions for yourself. You choose a college and/or profession. You may decide where and how you want to live, how much money you want to make and what you want to do with it, what kind of "lifestyle" you want to have. You have developed your personal identity to some extent. You may have sought adventure, taking an unusual vacation or working in an exotic location, doing something outside your comfort zone to test your limits. You may have developed career goals, dreams for life, and may have begun implementing them. You get your feet (fairly) firmly planted on the ground, and you're (somewhat) certain about the direction your life is going to take.

hen, you meet someone special. Or you suddenly realize that the "best buddy" you've had for years is really the love of your life. You fall in love. Your relationship grows, develops, and matures. You and your partner decide you want to get married. Then, you decide where and how you want to live, how much money you want to make, and what you want to do with it—oh, right, all those things we talked about in the previous paragraph, only now, you're planning for two.

You marry, and then you may decide to have children. Most likely, you and your spouse become the breadwinners and providers for your child or children. Your extended family may or may not be in a position— emotionally, geographically, or financially—to help. You shoulder the responsibilities associated with being a husband, wife, mother, and father.

Your children grow, and soon they become young adults. They may leave home, start their own careers and families, and never return. Or they may encounter challenges and come to live with you again, or need money.

But, finally, there is the expectation that, at some point, you and your spouse can come full circle: a place where it's just the two of you, with, hopefully, enough financial security to pursue your dreams, whether they include travel, a second career, or charitable activities, and, perhaps, spending time with your grandchildren.

With a few revisions here and there, we can all recognize the lives of many people we know in this overview. It's a fairly natural progression that's based on a combination of societal and cultural factors, economic factors, and the evolution of human development and behavior over time.

Like the growth and development of the human body, and, really, all of nature, the growth and development of a person takes time. You can't rush it. Well, you can, but the results may not be what you'd hoped for. At the age of four, a child needs to play with toys and not be told the harsh realities of life. At the age of 34, the toys should have been put away, and a very comprehensive understanding of the world and its ways should be firmly in hand. Cultures and families have their own ways of leading a person from childhood to adulthood, with educational institutions, sports, religious rituals, family traditions, social functions, and the like.

We participate in these, sometimes reluctantly, and they change us, usually for the better. We're thrown into an environment where we don't know things. We are taught by teachers, mentors, peers, and experience. We learn. We are tested. We are transformed. We graduate, and then we move on. We apply what we've learned directly to our professions, or we simply appreciate the process for what it has added to our overall quality of life. This happens in school, the military, religious orders, on-the-job training, self-improvement endeavors, and social clubs.

These experiences are the difference between an 18-year-old college freshman and a 22-year old college graduate. One is still pretty much a kid; the other can lay claim to some credibility as an adult. Entering the workforce and learning from those experiences for ten years, the 32-year-old who was once the college graduate should be even more mature.

Of course, people are individuals. Some are very mature at a very young age, and some never grow up. We've all seen that. But, on the whole, who is a better candidate to enter into marriage: the 18-year-old college freshman? Or the 32-year-old with a college degree and ten years of work experience under his (or her) belt?

The answer is obvious. Why? Because there are certain things that only time and experience can do. When things in life are rushed or a process is truncated prematurely, it may have repercussions later. If a young man goes straight from high school, for example, directly into the military, does his tour of duty, and then is honorably discharged, he may not immediately be ready to be an employee, a husband, and a father. The fact that he may want to live as a bachelor, a student, a ranch hand, or a backpacker in Europe for a year or two is no character flaw. He simply hasn't had the opportunity to be on his own for a period of time with no pressing responsibilities. He may need to let the dust settle, in a manner of speaking, before he's ready to move on to the next stage of his life.

If you're in the student or young adult phase of life, cutting that short because you want or have to get married can seriously impact your life and all of your relationships. This, too, is obvious, but it's worth stating. The list of things and people you may resent as a result can be a long one: you may resent your spouse for pressuring you into it; you may resent your parents and friends for not talking you out of it; you may resent your child for limiting your opportunities. That's no way to live.

To the extent that you fully experience each stage of life is probably going to be the extent that you fully enjoy all of life. When you're a child, be a child. Hopefully, events will not conspire to make your childhood traumatic or force you into the responsibility of adulthood prematurely. When you're a student, be a student. Study, laugh, learn, explore, question, challenge, dream. But don't rush into adulthood, if at all possible, by starting a family or getting married before you're prepared to.

Understand, honor, and respect nature and its processes. The stages of life that are a part of our existence are natural, sometimes slow, but critical to our success in life, love, and marriage. I've discussed the stages of life at the start of this book on marriage for several reasons.

Here they are:

- You have to know where you are before you can chart a course to go somewhere else;

- You have to articulate and acknowledge the path that you've taken, the journey you've experienced, and understand how it's affected and shaped you before you can credibly commit to another person for a lifetime; and

- You have to let go of your garbage in order to make room for your treasure.

The result that can come from this awareness is that you can sit down with your potential spouse and say, "This is how I grew up, what I experienced, how I think it impacted me, how I felt really blessed and then how I felt a little (or a lot) short-changed, and how I want to make sure that our life together absolutely has this in it and absolutely does not have this in it."

You'll be out of breath after that run-on sentence, but in saying it, you'll have done more to start your relationship off on solid ground than most couples. Some couples have haphazard conversations like this late at night, in the car, after making love, here and there, with varying amounts of real communication and understanding.

With an issue as important as marriage, I suggest that you write this stuff down. Ask your potential spouse to write it down. Then sit down in a dedicated space, and without interruption, discuss what you've written down. Even more importantly, listen to what your potential spouse has to say. If they tell you that their childhood was marred with anxiety about financial insecurity due to their parents' behavior, that's an important emotional issue that you will have to prioritize in order to make your marriage work.

So you'll be reading your list of how you grew up, what you experienced, and how you think it shaped you, but, more importantly, you'll be listening and writing down the things that are important to your potential spouse. If you can't listen to your potential spouse, understand what they're saying and how they feel about what they're saying, and make choices, and perhaps changes in your behavior, to show you're aware and that you care, you're not ready for marriage.

Again, if you can't listen to your potential spouse's important issues and honestly see yourself making choices or reaching a mutually satisfying arrangement or compromise to accommodate their feelings, then you're not ready to marry this particular person, no matter how much you love them right now.

During the life of your marriage, you're going to consistently make choices and take actions that put the feelings of your spouse first. Your spouse, in turn, is going to do the same for you. You're not going to have sex with other people. You're not going to spend money any way you please. You are going to make allowances for the behavior of family members, both yours and your spouse's. You're not going to abuse alcohol, drugs, your spouse, or your children. You're going to "have their back" and they're going to have yours. This is, to put it indelicately, the deal.

This is a long road and a lot of work, but it is beyond worth it in so many ways and on so many levels. The first thing you must do, however, is take an inventory of yourself. What you've been through and where you're at. Be honest with yourself first. Be honest with your potential spouse, too.

You do that by assessing what stage of life you're currently in, if you've ticked all the boxes in your previous stages, so to speak, so that you don't feel like you've missed out on anything. If you feel like you've done it all as a child, adolescent, or young adult, or if you truly feel alright about the things you didn't get to do, at that point, you might be ready for marriage.

Questions to ask and answer:

• What stage of life am I experiencing right now?

• Looking back, do I feel like any stage of my life was cut short? Was any stage extended too long, beyond what is healthy?

• Were these time periods a direct result of a choice I made? Or were these choices made by my family? Were these circumstances beyond anyone's control?

- Looking at my present situation, do I feel any resentment or see any repercussions that have resulted from a stage of my life not being fully experienced?

- Do I blame myself for the choices I made? Do I blame my family? Do I blame God?

- Is blaming anyone for anything helping me live a fuller life? Or is it holding me back?

- Can I fix or revisit an issue from a previous stage in my life that I feel I didn't experience fully? (For example, if your education was cut short due to a family obligation, can you now go back to school?)

- Can I let go of any and all resentment about a stage of my life not being fully experienced?

- Can I accept responsibility for what might happen in my life if I don't let go of these resentments?

- Can I change the past?

- Can I change the future, other than by making choices and taking action in the present moment?

◊ ◊ ◊ ◊

'Family' is a word loaded with emotion and contradiction. It is composed of its individual members, and yet it is a single unit. It has rules, and it is often ungovernable. Its members go their own way, but often cannot escape it. It makes the good times even better, and the bad times bearable.

It is composed of those we love more than life, and those we despise more than our worst enemies. It is also, magically, composed of those we didn't even know were there for us, as we'll learn in this blog post.

From *The Old Money Book* blog
July 21, 2016

Who Are You?

I received an email the other day from someone I did not know. It contained a single sentence.

"Who are you?"

Very quickly, my mind ran from Friedrich Nietzsche to Roger Daltry back to Carl Jung over to Hindu philosophy... Then I calmed myself, realized that this person was inquiring about who I was as it related to the content I share on this blog and in *The Old Money Book*, as well as *The Old Money Guide To Marriage*. Not a bad question.

Who am I? I'll tell you: I'm the uncle that your parents warned you about.

Perhaps you're just out of college. Perhaps you're attending the wedding of a cousin. You're at the reception, fairly bored, trying to avoid people of all ages who may want to dance with you or introduce you to someone who would be absolutely perfect for you.

So you grab onto the railing of the banquet room bar like it was a life preserver in the middle of an angry ocean. You sip a strong drink and hold tight, warily watching the crowd, but trying not to make eye contact with any of them.

I, who stand right next to you and have preceded your arrival at this oasis of alcoholic beverages by at least a half hour, feel the same way. I don't know these people and I probably don't like them. I may or may not be better than them, but I am certain I have little in common with them. The couple getting married are not so closely related that

I have to care, but not so distantly related that I could not attend without hearing about it at some point. So we have that misery in common.

My shirt and tie color combination make you blink, but the navy blazer and muted slacks compensate almost enough. My shoes may be the only thing you recognize as being really expensive. My hair is thin and grey. My eyes have dark circles around them. I'm not trying to be hip. We say hello and exchange pleasantries.

You realize that your parents have mentioned me, with the requisite roll of the eyes. "A snob." "A little eccentric." "Uses colorful language too frequently." "Doesn't play well with others." All true, I admit. I've made a couple of snarky remarks about the other guests, but I've also told you a story about your father's incredible generosity to a family member in need—that you didn't even know about—and you realize that I can be quite genuine, possibly generous, perhaps fun, and at least not as bad as I've been made out to be.

We discuss your plans for school and the future. I listen. I give you unvarnished advice on a couple of topics, and offer to keep in touch. The bride and groom head off for the honeymoon, and, gratefully, we can "blow this pop stand" (as we used to say back in the day) without fear of social or familial retribution.

A couple of weeks later, you're thinking about something. You don't have an answer. You don't want to ask your parents about it because they're your parents. They're in your head like a bad pop song all the time.

You send me an email. My reply is wicked, irreverent, but accurate and almost prescient. I've been there. I've heard it all, seen a lot of it, and done some of it. I've got my opinions but feel free to differ, and good luck with that. I'm not often wrong. But you can tell I care about you and I hope the best for you, whether it's regarding love or money or whatever.

Who am I? I'm your Uncle Byron. This blog and my books are my correspondence to you.

PRIVACY

"I made a hell of a lot of money, and a hell of a lot of mistakes, but all before the Internet came along. Thank God."
— *OMG from Boston, still wishing to remain anonymous*

The final, and perhaps most important core value of Old Money, is privacy.

It has been said that Old Money individuals who live appropriately have their names in the newspapers three times: when they're born, when they marry, and when they die.

In contrast, contemporary American culture is fame-obsessed, and it appears that the disease is contagious. The public equates fame with accomplishment, even accepting the acquisition of fame as an accomplishment unto itself. The internet has convinced people that others really care about what they do all day, that their opinions are worth considering, and that having the opportunity and ability to share information means that it should be shared.

We don't. They aren't. And you shouldn't.

Old Money lives discreetly. There are reasons for this. Discretion minimizes resentment from others. It minimizes requests for financial assistance from friends, relatives, and strangers. It minimizes attention from criminals, as well as would-be suitors who wish to marry into money. It assists in developing and maintaining healthy friendships with others who may have less money.

The lack of conspicuous consumption and haughty behavior helps Old Money and the public hold focus. The focus being that we are all human beings. We are all citizens of our particular city, nation, and world. While we may have more or less resources than others, we walk the same streets and contribute to—or detract from—the overall quality of life by our behavior. We do this in ways large and small. Old Money knows this. Old Money remembers this.

Old Money knows that sometimes, like it or not, others look to it to set an example, to set a standard, to deal with good fortune and bad with equanimity. Old Money knows that this is most easily done by focusing on work, family, and friends, and not fame.

Old Money may enter the entertainment industry or play professional sports. When it does, it usually excels at its endeavors. Poise and privacy are maintained. Family background is omitted or obscured whenever possible. The focus remains on the work. And when the show or the game is over, Old Money goes home.

Old Money saying: to live well, live in secret.

Make no mistake, Old Money lives well. It knows the wisdom and tranquility of not having everyone know everything. It knows how impressive it is when someone has done much and said little, if anything, about their accomplishments.

In matters of the heart, it is best to keep your affairs confidential. Do not kiss and tell. It will, inevitably, get back to the person in question. Such betrayals are almost impossible to repair. The number of people you have slept with is not an accomplishment to be proud of, for either sex. Do *text messages* and *explicit photos* need to be discussed?

In matters of finance, it is also best to keep your affairs confidential. Money is discussed with your family in private or with professionals, such as a CPA or money manager. It is uncouth to discuss your net worth, income, material possessions, or career position in a social setting. The only thing worse is discussing someone else's. Both scenarios reek of insecurity and tell the world you are a recent arrival to the moneyed class or an imposter.

If someone asks you a question you are not comfortable answering, you have options. You may say, "That's an interesting question. Why do you ask?" When they tell you why they want to know, you will have a clearer picture about their intentions and can decide on how to respond, if you decide to respond at all. "I'm sorry, that's not something I discuss," is a solid stock reply. Or, "I'm sorry. I can't answer that." Then, stop talking, change the subject, or excuse yourself politely and walk away.

Some clever people may ask, "What did you say you did for a living?" when they know full well you haven't mentioned it. Feel free to say, "I didn't." Americans have a bad habit of asking people what they do for a living upon an initial introduction. A good response to this is to keep your reply vague by saying, "I'm in the entertainment business," and continue by saying, "but my real passion is Egyptian history." Chances are the person will take the hint and ask you about Egyptian history. You can talk Tut briefly, and then ask them about their passion or interests.

Maintaining your privacy can be simple: don't talk about it; don't put it in writing; don't post it on the internet.

Helpful Hints

- If anyone tells you they're Old Money, they're not. Run, don't walk, away.

"Wow. I knew they had money, but I had no idea they had that much money." This is a frequent comment about people who suddenly realize their friends are Old Money.

- If you discover that your friend is Old Money, never mention it to your friend or anyone else. To do so risks the friendship.

• Be more. Seem less.

• A secret is not something you tell one person at a time.

• The personal information and photos you've posted online are there forever. This is something to consider when you think about new relationships, college applications, and job applications.

• Fame is like wearing a fur coat 365 days a year. And if you don't think it's fleeting, pick up a two-year-old copy of your favorite tabloid.

• You cannot control fame. You can control privacy.

• Don't do anything for the approval of anyone else, especially the public.

• Be careful what you share with others.

• Be careful who you invite to your residence.

• It's difficult for others to disrupt, sabotage, or voice their opinion about something they don't know about.

• Mystery is the new black. Conversation is also the new black.

• One poorly timed comment or action in public can destroy a reputation built over decades.

• Watching television is not preferable, but it is preferable to being watched by television.

• Just because someone with a microphone or camera asks you a question does not mean that you are required to answer.

• Get off Facebook. Get out. Spend time with real friends, face to face. Talk.

• Do not gossip. When someone else starts to, excuse yourself and step away.

• If you can avoid it, do not have your actual home address on your driver's license. Unless required, do not have your home address printed on your checks. Use a mail drop or post office box.

• If you are in a high-profile or controversial line of work, consider having cards printed with only your name and email address (perhaps a mobile phone number) on them. Give them to people you meet in social settings instead of your business card.

PRIVACY
That Was Then. This Is Now.

In 2020, a presence on social media is now considered essential for working people, with the possible exception of government spies. LinkedIn, Twitter, and other platforms provide exposure, drive commerce, and engender credibility in a hyper-competitive marketplace. Social media makes ambitious and talented people accessible to potential employers, clients, and colleagues. It also makes people crazy. They live on their phones and online. They can't hold a train of thought, much less a conversation. They have withdrawals if they can't check their "feed." We all know people like this. We just don't want to be people like this.

Sure, it's great to connect with friends effortlessly and instantly and "put yourself out there" professionally, but there is a danger that being in the digital world for prolonged periods impacts the ability to function in the real world. Attention spans are shortened. Anxiety levels are heightened. And the ability to articulate nuanced and complex ideas is impaired. Don't even get me started on punctuation and grammar, which seem to be optional in blog posts, emails, texts, and now business correspondence.

During the pandemic, the amount of daily "screen time" we all used to worry about went out the window. We were all shut in (or at least we were in France). There was nothing else to do except work, exercise, read a book, play music, or watch Netflix documentaries.

I sincerely believe life will soon be back to some sort of normal, and the time you spend tapping on your phone, scrolling on your laptop, and flicking channels on your television should be reduced significantly.

Real life is out there, and we all need to participate in it.

Your personal mental health is an obvious concern. There are societal dangers, as well. Informed individuals who study and implement social media marketing programs and strategies have called the techniques and algorithms used online "weapons grade technology." If you take a moment to digest that description, it's not a nice term. It's actually a very scary concept that is currently being used on you, and probably against us. *Us,* you know, the people who allegedly make up a democracy.

The persuasive abilities of social media feeds, ads on Facebook, and "news" on YouTube are alarmingly effective. They can send people down a rabbit hole. They can make people literally not believe facts that are presented to them in black and white. They can make people deny or doubt evidence presented by numerous reputable news organizations and/or qualified scientists. They can make people believe a pandemic is a hoax. These digital ringworms can rewire people's brains to reject realities that are understood to be true by a vast majority of sane, evidence-based thinkers who base their conclusions on logic and the obvious. It is a clear and present danger we all need to be aware of: if we can't be alone to contemplate our thoughts, we have lost our privacy.

My own experience with social media has been limited and unpleasant. I didn't like Facebook when I first learned about it, but I was persuaded for a short time to join it. I didn't like it for the period of time I was on it. They wanted to know too much about me. They wouldn't tell me why they wanted to know so much about me, or what they would do with the information they learned about me. It was also incredibly time-consuming. When I elected to delete my Old

Money Book Facebook account, they bid me farewell, then didn't delete the account. (It's still visible and neglected since 2018.)

And now that we've all learned the role Facebook played in the 2016 presidential election, my suspicions have been borne out: they, like many internet companies, want as much information about you as possible in order to sell that information to third parties. Those third parties will then use that information to sell you things, whether they be sweatshirts, weight loss products, or political candidates. They will shape your preferences and limit your choices by the way they present "search results."

They will present you with content and ads that are relevant to your hobbies and tastes, which might be helpful and enjoyable. But they will also bait you with content that they know angers you, then often present incrementally more extreme content on that particular subject, which is not helpful or healthy. They will monitor and record your every click on every ad, article, website, blog post, or video. They will track your every search, save, bookmark, purchase, comment, and like, and also *read the content of your personal emails* in order to learn more about your preferences, aspirations, and fears. If you let them, dear reader, they will know you better than you know yourself, and they will manipulate you.

I'm not being an alarmist. I'm echoing what numerous "disgruntled former employees" of big tech companies have said: the amount and the detail of what they know about us is dangerous. It's best to keep social media at arm's length. Use it for business if you must. Keep it compartmentalized if you can. Embrace it at your peril.

If you do not want something to be public, do not write it in an email, post it on social media, or say it over a telephone line. There is no such thing as "security" or "privacy" online. If online privacy is important to you, I would suggest the following:

• Use a paid email service with servers housed in Switzerland, where privacy laws are strict.

• Clear your cookies and caches after every session online. (If you don't know what these are, find out, then delete them regularly.)

• Use "incognito mode" when searching online, and don't use Google or Chrome; use DuckDuckGo and Firefox as your default search engine and browser.

• Don't put any more photos of yourself online. To understand why I say this, research the facial recognition software innovations currently being used and developed by governments and big tech.

• Delete all the online photos of yourself that you can.

• Close your Facebook account, please. Facebook is not your friend.

• Use a company like Signal instead of WhatsApp (owned by Facebook) for free phone calls and messaging.

• Put a piece of black tape over your laptop camera lens when not in use, and

• Uninstall Zoom and other video call applications after use. (They can still listen to you through the microphone on your laptop, even after your call has ended, if you don't.)

• Beware of TikTok, the popular video-sharing app. As of this writing, their track record on privacy and protecting underage users is questionable.

- For financial privacy, you might consider the following:

- Opening a bank account outside the United States in order to hold cash in a second currency and/or shield your assets from scrutiny. (You will want to declare these accounts to the IRS on your tax returns. Speak with your CPA.)

- Holding some of your assets in a trust (see a lawyer about this).

- Paying cash when you can and use credit or debit cards only when you must.

- Not using your mobile phone to pay for goods or services. With your banking or credit card information on a portable, vulnerable device, you increase your chances of being the victim of fraud.

- Learning more about the "Own Your Data" movement and participate as you feel appropriate.

Of course, there are many resources online that offer tips and tricks about how you maintain and regain your privacy. Of course, you'll be searching for that information online...so, you know, beware.

◊ ◊ ◊ ◊

When we talk about privacy, we think mostly about ways we can protect ourselves. We rarely think about the ways we can protect others. That is, however, exactly what diplomats think about and do. So much of the time their work is done behind closed doors. Once in a while, though, we learn about their efforts, and how much impact they have in our world. Below, I share one of those moments.

From *The Old Money Book* blog
February 7, 2020

Saving Paris

Recently, I was invited for drinks at the Swedish Club, a private club in Paris. A friend who enjoys a membership there was in town from the states, and the evening provided us some quiet time to catch up.

Members of the secluded, security-heavy club seem to be a mélange of aristocrats, diplomats, international businessmen (my friend), a few artists, and the odd writer or two.

The atmosphere was elegant but relaxed. The drinks were priced reasonably. Live jazz drifted from the main room, past the dining room, and into the cozy bar, where my friend and I sequestered ourselves in a corner.

The architecture was classically French, with period details gracing the pale aqua colored walls and 15-foot ceilings. A hundred-year-old dinner-plate-sized clock was set into the brown marble fireplace on one wall. Neither was working, but it mattered not: no one has any pressing engagements after 9 pm in Paris, and fireplaces in the city are no longer permitted to burn wood.

Busts of famous Swedes and stacks of books on a variety of subjects crowded the shelves of the room. A massive rack of moose antlers loomed over the mirrored bar, looking down on framed portraits, landscapes, and maps.

The club has a history, of course. One of the more memorable moments was during World War II. The Nazis occupied the French capital, but Allied forces were closing in. Retreat was inevitable for the German forces, but Hitler was not letting his army leave without making a statement.

He had ordered the German commander in charge of the city to rig every bridge, every important monument, and every cultural landmark in Paris with explosives. Once the German army retreated across the last remaining bridge and headed back to Germany, the plan went, the explosives would be set off.

The result would be that the Eiffel Tower, Notre Dame, the Louvre, the Opera—every iconic building or landmark that makes Paris what it is—would be destroyed. The bridges would be demolished, damming the Seine and sending waters overflowing into the streets. Some Parisians would instantly drown. Many more would suffer and die of disease, as drinking water, food, and medical supplies would be interrupted and disrupted for weeks or even months.

It was a monstrous plan that only Hitler could have come up with. Upon receiving intelligence that the Allied forces were approaching, the German general was fully prepared to follow orders. The explosives were in place. All that remained was for the Nazis to evacuate, and the final command to be given. Paris would be destroyed.

A Swedish diplomat, however, learned of the plan. He approached the general and, over the course of two fraught and perilous weeks, persuaded him not to go through with it. (I will not divulge all the details. Watch the wonderful French film *Diplomacy* online and enjoy...)

The two men held their tense, emotional conversations at the Swedish Club, in the bar.

After the war, the French government sent a message to the retired Swedish diplomat. They wanted to see him. They also communicated the same message to the now-defeated and retired German general. It seemed that the request for their presence was, well, not really a request.

Dutifully, and perhaps a little nervously, the two men arrived in Paris. And, in a ceremony that could only have been conceived and executed by the French, they were both given France's highest military honor, the *Croix de guerre avec palme*, in recognition of their service to Paris.

PART II

How Old Money Does It

ATTIRE

"What a strange power there is in clothing." – Isaac Bashevis
Singer

Nothing tells others more about you than the way you dress. You can deride the statement as a symptom of a superficial world, but that does not change the fact that it is true. Clothes protect us from the elements and prevent us from being arrested for public indecency. They are also a means of expression: your profession, your aspirations, your background, your self-image, all of this and more are expressed to others by your clothes. Others will, upon first encountering you, take a visual inventory of your appearance and consciously or subconsciously assign certain personality traits and values to you, whether you possess them or not. This will work to your advantage or disadvantage, depending on the way you dress.

Clothes are used to convey authority and sexual prowess as well as financial position and social status. They reveal what culture or class we belong to, or desire to belong to. Therefore, to understand Old Money, you must understand how it dresses and why.

For Old Money, what is worn is almost without exception what is appropriate to wear for a particular occasion, what looks good (i.e., classic, timeless style), and what is comfortable. Clothing is generally not worn to call attention to oneself. Discretion is paramount. Fashion is to be avoided like the plague. Classic styles in natural fabrics form a roster of reliable, top-quality garments that constitute the majority of the Old Money wardrobe. Value, comfort, and quality are the watchwords here.

Old Money saying: it should take someone five minutes to realize that you're well-dressed.

Old Money dresses in a generally low-key way because they have no need or desire to call attention to the fact that they have money, status, or privilege. But that does not mean that they do not dress well. Quite the contrary. But there is a difference between dressing well and dressing fashionably. Everyone else buys "the latest fashion" advertised in magazines, worn by supermodels or celebrities. Everyone else pays retail for these garments of generally questionable quality. Everyone else is seduced by "bargains" they see advertised. Generally these goods are not of good quality, and will be "out of fashion" next year. Everyone else's money will have been wasted, or at the very least not used as well as it could have been.

Note: cheap clothing purchased by many people has a negative global impact. The working conditions and wages for people making a T-shirt that retails for $5 are almost always appalling. In fact, they are generally slave-like. Think about it: it's the only way to make a profit on an item sold at such a low retail price. Furthermore, the increase in the purchase of cheap clothing by Western populations influences farmers in developing countries; they stop growing food to feed themselves and their local communities and start growing cotton to sell to mills and garment manufacturers. As cotton is the most pesticide-intensive crop in the world, cheap clothing made from it impacts the environment as well.

Old Money, on the other hand, buys quality clothes, traditionally styled, and wears them for decades. Old Money dresses. Everybody else dresses up or barely gets dressed at all.

Old Money always looks presentable. Shirts, blouses, skirts, and pants are pressed; well-made and well-cared-for shoes are worn. Hair is combed and clean. A certain benchmark is met, even in the most casual of settings.

If you dress like Old Money, no one will really notice how you dress. No one will know how much money you have or don't have. They will only assume that you have taste and discretion. Not bad things to be known for.

Attire for the Old Money Guy

Entire books have been written for men about dressing well. Print magazines and the internet are full of advice. There are discussions of fabrics, colors, collar styles, and lapel widths. In some instances these are well-written and helpful. In other instances, they are just a not-so-subtle form of advertising and ignorant chatter.

Following Madison Avenue's ever-changing advice on fashion can be too expensive and time-consuming for the man who may be (or should be) committing his resources and attention elsewhere. Following Old Money's advice, which is most often conveyed by example, will serve a man well, whether he's just starting out or starting over.

The Old Money Guy focuses on quality and value, simplicity and comfort. This starts with shoes. Quality shoes in brown or black are the foundation, literally, of an enduring wardrobe. Consider Allen Edmonds shoes, which are made in America, generally traditional in style, and durable. Lace-up wing tips or cap toe shoes are suitable for business. Penny loafers are perfect for casual wear. You'll want cedar shoe trees for these, as they'll help retain the shape of the shoe, minimize the damage caused by moisture, and extend their life. Deck shoes (Sperry Topsiders) are a staple for school or weekends, with jeans or khakis. Sneakers should be worn when playing sports or during leisure activities only.

When you are ready to buy clothes the way the OMG buys clothes, go to Brooks Brothers, Ralph Lauren, or J. Press and explain your situation to a salesman there. Tell him you want to start or add to your wardrobe by purchasing *quality items that will not go out of style*. Then listen to him. Look at him. Is he dressed in a traditional, classic style? Or is he a preppy wannabe? Be circumspect. You may have $5,000 to spend or $500. The right salesperson will be willing to work with you and guide you. Do not be shy: ask about upcoming sales or discounts. You're investing. Purchase slowly. Consider where and when you will wear each item you consider buying. Right now you're buying for every day or at least every week. Purchase for year-round wear when buying suits, jackets, or slacks, if possible.

A traditionally tailored solid navy or dark gray suit is a staple of the OMG wardrobe. Black is a little too severe and brown is more appropriate for sport coats. This suit will be worn for job interviews, work, religious services, elegant evening events, weddings, and funerals (other people's and your own). The style is such that it would not be noticeably different than something worn 50 years ago. Lapels and shoulders are neither too narrow nor too wide. Pants are neither too slim nor too baggy. The fabric is a year-round wool. The suit has a silk lining of a dark color. It will be only slightly tailored to your body by the tailor at Brooks Brothers, Ralph Lauren, or J. Press. If it needs serious tailoring, it's not the right size or it's not the right suit.

If you find a quality suit at a discount or department store, be careful. Their tailors may not be up to the job. In all likelihood you will need to find a tailor elsewhere to alter the suit jacket and pants you purchase off the rack. You will find this person in an Old Money neighborhood, probably in a small shop. For a small amount of money, he will make you and your suit look good. The price/quality range for an off-the-rack suit at the above-mentioned establishments runs from a few hundred dollars to a bespoke number from Anderson and Sheppard in London for several thousand dollars. Yes, Old Money likes bespoke.

Note: Old Money does not wear a business suit to an event designated "black tie." A dinner jacket with bow tie is worn to a black-tie event. Very good tuxedos, as they are also known, are available to rent in most cities. You will need to acquire a formal shirt. It should be white with French cuffs. It will not have ruffles. If you wear a tuxedo less than four times a year, rent. If it's more than four times a year, consider a purchase. Rental houses have a good selection and put them on sale often. Retail establishments put them on sale just after the holidays. The jacket collar should be a shawl lapel or a peaked lapel, not a notched lapel, regardless of what anyone tells you. Only black shoes are worn with a tuxedo. The tuxedo is always black. Learn to tie a bow tie: ladies love pulling the knot loose at the end of a wonderful evening (wink, nod).

The long-sleeve 100% cotton shirt worn with the suit is white or light blue. The shirts can be a pinpoint collar or a button-down collar for a slightly less formal look. Brooks Brothers, Ralph Lauren, L.L. Bean, Land's End, Mercer and Sons, Hamilton, and J. Press all make quality shirts at a variety of price points. Start with them. Develop your preferences; mind your budget. Later on in life and success, Charvet in Paris makes the finest bespoke shirts in the world for the OMG that likes that luxury.

The silk ties, wherever they come from, are navy blue (the most formal), a red or dark green, or a regimental stripe with these colors. Avoid clever ties at this point, I beg you. The belt should match the shoes, black or brown, and be simple cow leather. No big buckles, no exotic skins. Socks are navy, black, or brown.

The go-to garment for the Old Money Guy is the navy blazer. The blazer can be single- or double-breasted. It is generally medium-weight wool. It's slow to wrinkle. It is versatile, worn with khakis, wool slacks that are grey or tan, or jeans. It is welcome at garden parties, graduations, dinner at home or out, and many business functions. With a tie, you are dressed appropriately for almost any occasion. Worn without a tie, you are still well-dressed. The shirts worn with this blazer are the same blue and white shirts worn with the suit. Brooks Brothers makes the iconic model. Quality blue blazers are made and sold the world over. Knock yourself out. Note: do not wear suit pants with a blazer.

Other odd jackets that serve the OMG well include the brown or grey tweed for winter, the brown or navy corduroy for fall, and the wheat or blue linen sport coat for spring and summer. Cashmere is for sweaters and scarves only, not jackets, and is a fundamental luxury later in life.

The OMG washes and irons his own shirts. No starch, please. You, old chap, will wash the shirts and let them hang dry on wooden hangers if you really want them to last. Run them through the dryer for a softer feel, but be prepared for accelerated wear if you do.

Sweaters are either wool or cotton at this point. Navy blue is a safe start. Cardigan, V-neck, or crew neck. They are worn over the same white and blue cotton shirts that are worn with the suit and the blazer.

Pullover polo shirts of 100% cotton in any color, but mostly solid colors, are worn for casual events or weekends. These are preferable to T-shirts, which are technically underwear, and last years longer. Ralph Lauren and Brooks Brothers make quality polos.

A London Fog trench coat and a Barbour jacket will serve you well if you live in colder, wetter climates. Navy blue, tan, or brown.

White, brown, tan, navy blue. Cotton, wool. Classic design. Quality fabrics. Don't try to reinvent the wheel, as any attempt to do so would be made in public.

Is the logic in all this becoming apparent? The OMG gives others the impression by the way he dresses that he is reliable and intelligent, that he has taste, and that he has no need to impress. He enjoys the benefits of convenience, comfort, classic style, and saving money.

Exceptions to this rule: Turnbull and Asser bespoke dress shirts and neckties in color combinations that will scorch the retina, but, thankfully, are worn under dark, conservative blazers and suit jackets by older OMGs; and madras sport coats or pants, usually in an obnoxiously colorful check that can be seen from outer space, but thankfully are only worn during the summer, usually by younger OMGs.

Note: Old Money is to preppy what an oil painting is to a cartoon.

Note: the OMG wears a shirt. The belly of the OMG is seen by his spouse and his doctor, unless he is wearing a bathing suit, which is worn at the beach or the pool only. When traveling, a shirt or robe is worn going to and from the hotel swimming pool.

Grooming for Men

Cleanliness is essential for Old Money. Fingernails are trimmed and clean. Hygiene is paramount. Body odor is unacceptable.

Shaving is a ritual, practiced every work day and most weekends.

Facial hair is tricky. Know thyself.

Old Money goes gray. Old Money goes bald.

Tattoos and piercings: if you have to ask, you're reading the wrong book.

Jewelry for Men

Wedding ring. Class ring (from a university). Thin gold watch on leather strap. Maybe a stainless steel Rolex. Stop.

For Reference

Dressing the Man, by Alan Flusser, is an excellent book on how to dress well. Its historic perspective and detailed, almost

THE OLD MONEY BOOK

encyclopedic volume of information leave nothing to chance. It also includes many fascinating photos of well-dressed, Old Money men.

The Relationship

A local craftsman who can preserve and repair your shoes as needed. This includes repair and replacement of heels and soles, not just polishing.

A local tailor who can alter and repair garments as needed. This tailor may also make bespoke clothing, which you may acquire later in life.

Attire for Old Money Gals

Women have historically placed more importance on their attire than men. Therefore, the simple and straightforward approach with which we addressed Old Money attire for men may be inadequate when we address Old Money attire for women.

Nevertheless, it is important to note that many Old Money Gals (OMG again!) go to Brooks Brothers or Ralph Lauren, purchase oxford cloth button down dress shirts, wool or cotton sweaters, wool or khaki pants and skirts, and blue blazers that mirror their male counterparts and look just fine in them. They wear this style with complete confidence, contentment, and aplomb from cradle to grave and never give it a second thought. If you can dress this way and feel good about it, do so. You'll save money in the long run. In a world where so many chase after the latest trend to stand out from the crowd, ironically, you could be viewed as having a unique style.

That said, some OMGs require a little more continental flair in their wardrobe, but they still adhere to classic styles, quality fabrics of cotton, silk, and wool, and well-made garments purchased at reasonable prices. For them, too, garments are purchased and worn for decades without concern for "fashion." Designer labels hold no sway over them; they search for a quality garment at a good price, period. They know where, when, and how often they will wear a piece prior to purchasing it. They buy classic pieces and know that most everything they have can be worn with most everything else.

Inevitably, some pieces will, over time, become dated. Old Money Gals donate these items to their favorite charity, get a receipt for the donation, and write it off on their taxes.

For OMGs working outside the home, the first order of wardrobe business is the business suit. This suit is conservatively cut, made of a year-round wool that is slow to wrinkle, and is best in navy blue, charcoal grey, or black. The shoulders are not excessively padded. The skirt is just below the knee (preferred) or barely above it. If the skirt has a slit to make it more comfortable, the slit is in the back, not on the thigh.

A similar suit composed of a jacket and pants may be worn, depending on the occupation and the culture, but this is a more casual business suit. When in doubt, err to the conservative. Later in life, you may have the option of owning a classic Chanel suit, which OMGs positively wear into the ground.

This business suit is worn with a white blouse made of cotton or silk, which may be long sleeve or short. The more formal is a long-sleeve blouse. The blouse should be cut and worn as not to reveal cleavage. The pantyhose worn with this suit are a neutral color, navy, or black, and do not attract undue attention. No comment will be made on *fishnet stockings*.

The shoes worn with this business suit, white blouse, and conservative hose are simple, classic, mid-height leather pumps of navy blue or black with a closed toe.

Another business option for women is a pair of wool or linen slacks, cotton or silk blouse, and a wool or linen blazer. Again, the slacks are best in navy blue, black, brown, charcoal, tan, and dark green. White is for summer, unless it's a winter white, and is not generally acceptable in a business setting. Blouses should be a solid color, with white and light blue leading the way. The wool or linen blazer is tan, brown, or navy blue.

The go-to garment for the Old Money Gal is the classic black dress. It is a one-piece garment of a classic style, usually a scoop neck and sleeveless, with or without a belt. It is never too short or too tight. It looks great and works well for a number of functions. It is worn by the OMG at festive cocktail parties, somber funerals, the opera (festive or somber), and elegant dinners in or out. A colorful shawl or black jacket can be thrown around the shoulders. A string of inherited pearls is often seen around the neck. Black pumps with a medium to high heel finish off the look. The OMG wears it and rests easy. She looks good. So will you (wink, nod).

Again, the Old Money Gal leans toward Ralph Lauren and Brooks Brothers for clothing for the same reason the Old Money Guy does: the clothes are good quality and never go out of style. If you're just starting out or starting over, consider building your wardrobe with these two establishments in mind. You may have limited funds, so there's no sense wasting them on less-than-quality garments that may look dated or wear out before their time. Watch for sales and find the location of the outlet stores in your area.

Stores like Banana Republic, the Gap, and Nordstrom follow the whims of fashion to some extent, but they have classic quality clothing available as well. It's just a matter of finding the right piece at the right price. Ask yourself: could this item have been worn 50 years ago and still looked good? Is the quality such that I could be wearing this item 50 years from now? If your answer to this "50/50" question is yes on both counts, you may have found a great addition to your wardrobe.

Shoes, purses, belts, and scarves are the time-tested way to inject life into the same basic outfits. Save your money and watch diligently for top-quality, classic pieces that are on sale. Your shoes, purses, and belts should be leather, not something that might be leather in its next life. Your scarves should be silk, not synthetic fabric. Thrift stores or charity shops adjacent to affluent neighborhoods are great places to pick these up at bargain prices. Find and frequent these stores often but keep your budget in mind.

For those living in colder climates, a full-length wool coat in a classic style and solid color—again think navy blue, grey, or black—is essential. A classic trench coat is, too. Consider London Fog's iconic model.

Leather boots in black or brown are also essential. When you consider a pair, think about ice, snow, and gravity, and stick with a low heel. Ankle boots are great, but boots that cover the calf will keep you warm when you're making the daily commute in a wool skirt. Keep the embellishments such as buckles and designs to a minimum on these boots. They are to keep your legs and feet warm and dry.

For weekends and casual events, polo shirts and oxford cotton shirts worn with conservatively cut jeans, khakis, and cotton or linen skirts serve the OMG well. The shirts can be fitted or loose, according to taste and the event. In the winter, turtleneck sweaters and corduroy pants abound. The black turtleneck with black wool pants is an easy and iconic winter look and great for holiday parties.

Exceptions to the rule: vibrant and colorfully patterned blouse paired with solid color pants. Or the other way around. These look fabulous in the spring and summer.

Wear sneakers and athletic apparel only when you are exercising.

Grooming for Women

Your hair should be cut and styled simply, so that you look your best with a minimum of daily effort. If you color your hair, the color should closely match your natural color. This means you may be a brunette, blond, or redhead, but not a blue or purple head.

The older you get, the shorter you should wear your hair.

Color, condition, and cut your hair on a regular basis. Do not let yourself go.

Your makeup should consist of a little mascara, a little eye shadow, and a little lipstick. Stop there. Foundations and rouges look artificial and can clog the pores. If you want rosy cheeks, exercise regularly. If you want clear, clean, and healthy skin, cut out the fast food, coffee, soft drinks, and cigarettes.

Use organic castor oil that is cold-pressed and cold-processed. Apply it to your face nightly. It will minimize wrinkles and pull the blood to the surface of the skin, creating a natural and healthy glow. No amount of makeup in the world will compensate for a destructive lifestyle and excess stress. To look good, live good.

Protect your skin. Moisturize with natural products that are not necessarily expensive. Moisturize from the inside out: take essential oils as dietary supplements when you take your vitamins. Dry brush your entire body. This removes dead skin and increases cardiovascular function as it pulls the blood to the surface.

Go easy on the cosmetic surgery. Limit your exposure to the sun. Overexposure causes wrinkles and can lead to disease.

Jewelry for Women

Less is more. Less is more. Less is more. This is not a typographical error.

If you are married, a simple wedding band in 18 karat gold or platinum speaks volumes.

If you have the cash, consider a Cartier Tank watch that will last you a lifetime. Used models are available in resale shops and online at surprisingly affordable prices. The simpler, the better. The iconic model has a white face, black Roman numerals, and black leather strap.

It's more impressive if each piece of jewelry has a story behind it. This gives each piece meaning to you when you wear it and to others when they ask about it. A Cartier watch might have been purchased at an antique shop during your first trip to Florence. An old gold ring might have been inherited from a beloved aunt. Adopting this strategy regarding jewelry will curb consumer-style spending at retail establishments and help you see each piece of jewelry as a touchstone for a memory, not a display of disposable income. Memories take time to accumulate and have value. So should jewelry.

When you or your spouse are ready to seriously accumulate quality pieces of jewelry, do not pay retail for new jewelry at brand-name establishments that advertise in newspapers, magazines, and on television. You will be paying for that advertising, as well as premium retail overhead, when you buy the ring, necklace, earrings, or pendant. If you feel compelled to ignore this advice, then please go to Tiffany's and purchase something simple and platinum that's within your budget.

If you're not going to inherit pieces of jewelry, which is always preferable (wink, nod), seek out reputable family-owned dealers in small shops who sell antique and estate jewelry in your area, or in an affluent area near you. You may also want to investigate auctions being conducted in your area, a topic which is covered in detail in the "Furnishings" section of this book. You will get much more for your money buying estate pieces than buying new at retail.

If you consider purchasing pre-owned jewelry from a private party, take precautions: quality counterfeit goods are sold everywhere by a variety of reputable-looking people. Agree with the seller to have the piece of jewelry verified for authenticity by a reputable estate jewelry dealer in your area. It's a good idea to get a referral, visit a shop, and develop a relationship with a dealer prior to considering a purchase. This practice will save you plenty of heartache, even if the seller is a friend. They may not even know themselves that the piece they are selling is not genuine. This could double your trouble.

When you have been very successful, and you begin to consider high-quality watches for you or your spouse, keep the best company. The short list of watch brands which can be purchased used and which hold or increase in value over time includes: Rolex, Cartier, Patek Philippe, Audemars Piguet, IWC, Chopard, and Breguet.

In keeping with the Old Money philosophy, please have your family's financial future set before investing heavily in jewelry. Purchased correctly and properly maintained, these timepieces can be worn with pleasure, then handed down to the next generation.

Note: each ear may be pierced once in order to hold earrings. Nothing else should be pierced or tattooed, no matter how socially acceptable you may think it is or where it is located on your body.

Helpful Hints

If you think the oxford cloth button down shirt is too conservative for your tastes, try a white one on and turn the sleeves and collar up. Look in the mirror. Well, well...(wink, nod).

- Unless you are wearing a bathing suit and you are at the beach or the swimming pool, your stomach should not be visible.

- Your pants should not reveal the crack of your butt or your underwear. Your skirts should not be too short, and we all know how to measure that length.

- Wear a bra, even if nature has blessed you with the ability not to wear one and still look good.

- White jeans look best on slender women.

- Take pictures of yourself in the mirror to see what looks good on you. The camera doesn't lie. Delete the photos once you've made a determination.

- Not too baggy, not too tight. If you lose weight, good for you, but get those slacks taken in. If you gain weight, figure out why and alter your clothes so they fit. Then get busy with the exercise.

• Ask yourself: "What kind of attention do I want to attract?" Dress accordingly.

• If you can't walk in the shoes, don't wear the shoes.

• Do not purchase or accept as a gift counterfeit luxury items. The organized crime organizations that manufacture and distribute these items often use child and slave labor to produce them. These organizations may also engage in drug trafficking, prostitution, and human trafficking. What's more, Old Money can recognize an original, both in purses and people. Be that. Buy that.

• Find your style and embrace it.

For Reference

Chic Simple Dress Smart for Women by Kim Johnson Gross and Jeff Stone offers solid advice about the workplace wardrobe.

Study photographs of the late Jacqueline Kennedy Onassis and First Lady Michelle Obama. Look at their styles and incorporate them into your own.

The Relationship

A local seamstress who can alter and even create classic clothing for you is invaluable as you build and maintain your wardrobe. If she works from her home, that's even better. You will save money, and you'll have clothes that fit and flatter.

A hairstylist who knows your hair and can advise on what cut and color is most flattering.

A fashion designer whose style of clothes for women works on your body and clicks with your personal style is important. You may not buy his or her line exclusively, but you will have it in your mind when you shop. This will give your wardrobe a unified look, make mixing and matching items easy, and allow you to present a consistent, stylish image to the public every day.

ATTIRE
That Was Then. This Is Now.

Thankfully, not much has changed concerning Old Money attire. It is still a matter of dressing appropriately for the occasion, whether you're an Old Money Gal or an Old Money Guy.

Since the publication of *The Old Money Book*, I have written *Old Money, New Woman: How To Manage Your Money and Your Life*, and *Old Money Style: The Gentleman's Edition*. Both of these books go into detail about the philosophy and fundamentals of dressing well for the long haul. And by long haul, I mean adopting and enjoying an approach to clothing that is traditional in style, enduring in quality, and versatile in use.

Make no mistake: three years in Paris have not left me immune to the seductive powers of elegance and luxury. I encourage you to triumph over this pandemic, thrive in the new economy, and enjoy the fruits of your labor. However, obtain a certain level of financial independence first. Then reward yourself.

When you've paid off that student debt, enjoy a delicious dinner out on the town. When you've landed that new job, pop a bottle of champagne and toast with friends. When you have six months' living expenses saved in cash, splurge on that purse or sport coat you've been lusting for. Just make sure that it has the quality construction and timeless design that warrants the price for what some here in France call a "lifetime piece." Work hard. Spend wisely. Enjoy life.

Old Money Gals: learn how to curate a wardrobe. Avoid buying individual garments, shoes, and accessories at random. Old Money Guys: again, during this challenging time I encourage you to stick with the fundamentals of "The Uniform" and upgrade your wardrobe in subtle, but important ways: ditch the T-shirts and opt for pullover polo shirts; scrap the hoodie and sport a sweater; lose the ragged jeans and slip into some cotton pants.

Everybody, let your clothes work for you. Put your best foot forward on a daily basis. You're worth it.

Remember: if you buy the best, you only cry once.

As a final note on this subject, I really have to encourage you to avoid "fast fashion," i.e., cheap clothing that's being introduced to consumers on a massive scale almost every week. Huge retailers and brands launch these campaigns that feature the typical $10 top with $20 matching pants that are oh-so-comfortable and oh-so-chic and oh-so-affordable. It's tempting because you could literally purchase a new outfit every week, which is exactly what these retailers want you to do.

The problem with this business model is that the workers who produce a garment that you can purchase for $10 have been paid pennies to produce it. They're often working in slave-like conditions. The volume of natural resources and unnatural chemicals that go into producing this instantly disposable piece of clothing are enormous. The impact on our planet is not good and not small.

If you do not purchase these cheap garments, this business model will fail. Garment workers will have better chances of being paid fairly and working in safe conditions. As less water, cotton, and petroleum are being used to create these disposable products, Earth will have a chance to heal. And you'll look better because you'll be wearing quality clothing, even if you paid a little more for it.

Embrace sustainable fashion whenever you can. Avoid fast fashion always. Look for alternatives to leather. Leather tanning is an often toxic and always labor-intensive process that uses over 250 chemicals including heavy metals such as chromium, aldehyde, cyanide, zinc, and lead. None of these toxins are good for the people doing the tanning. They aren't good for the environment that absorbs the waste products created in the process, either.

As designers and consumers, we do have options, thanks to the dedicated efforts of visionary entrepreneurs like Dr. Carmen Hijosa. A former leather goods consultant, Dr. Hijosa saw the need for a natural, sustainable leather alternative, and Pinatex was born.

Pinatex is a material created from pineapple fiber, the byproduct of the annual pineapple harvest. Compared to traditional leather tanning, the production of Pinatex uses much less water and leaves behind much less waste after it's made. It also contains no animal products and no toxins. What's more, it looks great and feels fantastic.

Dr. Hijosa researched and developed her concept and presented it at a PhD exhibition at The Royal College of Art in London. Shortly thereafter, she founded Ananas Anam, Ltd., the company which today manufactures and distributes Pinatex worldwide.

I know we all love a great looking pair of leather shoes or a supple leather handbag. Still, we have to look for new ways to keep our style up and our carbon footprint down. To accomplish these goals, we have to seek out and support entrepreneurs like Dr. Hijosa who are doing well while doing good.

Now, for the Old Money Gals, I've included some wardrobe fundamentals detailed in *Old Money, New Woman*, below. Following that, there's an excerpt from *Old Money Style* in which I discuss the philosophy and purpose behind the gentleman's wardrobe.

And, of course, entertaining and insightful blog posts for all OMGs await you.

Enjoy.

From *Old Money, New Woman...*

Wear It Well

We've discussed Preparation. We've discussed Comportment. The final aspect of Presentation is your appearance: "Clothing and Grooming." The combination of these three aspects of Presentation is key as you prepare for this journey. This part of the package is no less important; it is simply the most visible.

Clothing and grooming are the first things a person notices when they meet you. Psychologists tell us that a person will make about a dozen visual observations and judgments in the first few seconds of meeting another person. That means, when someone is introduced to you for the first time, before you ever say a word, they've taken in and interpreted more than ten visual signals about you based on your appearance. They've looked at how you've dressed, if you've made any effort to dress, how tastefully you've executed that effort, and how appropriately dressed you are for the occasion. They will also consider how well or how poorly you've done your hair and makeup, the neatness and quality of your clothes, and your posture and composure.

These observations are then interpreted, given meaning and value, and then, like it or not, conclusions are drawn about you. It is probably unfair, but it is certainly true: people do judge a book by its cover, and a person by their appearance. The people you meet will equate the effort you've put into your appearance as being roughly equivalent to:

- the amount of respect you have for yourself;

- the respect you have for them and the value you've assigned to meeting them; and/or

- the importance you assign the event at which this meeting takes place.

To make the most of these moments, it is important to objectively assess how you look, not just to yourself in the mirror, but to others in public. Your journey to discover the best way to present yourself will be to find the "look" that is "you," whatever the occasion.

You'll identify and refine this "look" more quickly, easily, and less expensively if you know your body and know what looks good on you, without regard to passing trends or fads. Look at photos from your past. Critique your look from a year ago, five years ago, ten years ago. Again, find the look that works for you and refine it.

There are some inevitable basics to this process. They include quality, well-maintained clothes and shoes, a good haircut without a wild style-and-dye job, and a classic manicure—fingernails neither neglected nor overdone.

A key *Old Money, New Woman* fundamental of "dressing well" is "dressing appropriately." This is simply to know that what you wear is usually contingent upon the event you'll be attending or the activity you'll be participating in.

Before we go into detail, a final point: when you dress, it is important to consider your wardrobe as an *ensemble*. *Ensemble* is the French word for *together,* by the way. So if you want to look like you have it "together," view the articles of clothing you wear as team members. An Old Money Gal knows that this team, coordinated from head to toe, will work together to project a single image, one that makes a good *presentation* and one that is *appropriate* for the occasion.

Right Place, Right Time

With these ideas in mind, let's consider some familiar scenarios, or occasions, with some go-to ensembles that are appropriate for each.

The Professional Job Interview...in which the goal is to get hired and progress in your career. If you show up for a job interview at a major corporation in jeans and a too-tight sweater, it probably doesn't matter what credentials you have. The human resources executive is going to feel like you don't place any value on the meeting, or that you don't have a clue. Either way, they won't take the time to consider you seriously. They won't consider you at all.

Remember that, although corporate dress codes have been relaxed on "casual Fridays" at some companies, dress codes for interviews remain formal. Professional standards still apply. In the same way, appropriate interview attire for a company may differ from the day-to-day attire worn by employees in the office of that company. Just because employees dress in "business casual" attire when they arrive at work doesn't mean you show up in "business casual" for a job interview.

This scenario is the domain of the navy, black, or dark grey business suit with a skirt. Some women will wear suits with pants. Know your industry and the company you're interviewing with before ditching the skirt and wearing the pants. A white blouse and black or navy closed-toe heels or pumps complete the look.

*A Casual Social Event...*in which the goal is catch up with friends and meet new people—building relationships and having fun. If you show up at an afternoon neighborhood pool party in a short black dress, blown-out hair, industrial-strength mascara, and stilettos, you may garner some initial attention from the male attendees, but probably not the kind you want. You haven't dressed appropriately for the occasion. Other guests will probably think you're one brick shy of a load, or that you've taken on a new profession, at least part time. As with all Clothing and Grooming choices, know the event, know the host, know the crowd.

The Casual Lunch Out is the time and place for a cotton or linen blouse, a men's tuxedo shirt, cotton or linen pants or khakis, and casual shoes. Bring a sweater or shawl in case the restaurant is really proud of their air conditioning. Casual shoes are not athletic shoes. Flats or elegant, simple pumps are better than sandals and much preferred to ghastly flip-flops or clunky Birkenstocks. (Please, say "No" to Uggs.) Jeans are acceptable if they are not torn and don't reveal too much. Wear a heel to dress them up. Showing skin between your blouse and your pants should be reserved for the lake, the beach, or poolside at a resort.

The Backyard Barbecue, at a residence in the daylight hours, is perfect for a simple cotton or linen summer top, with cotton or linen pants (long or short), jeans, and some casual sandals or flats. Again no sneakers, flip-flops, or Birkenstocks, and again a sweater, if you need it when the sun goes down.

The Important Introduction is slightly more formal. A day-time example...Let's say you arrive to meet your boyfriend's parents for the first time. You've dressed in a clean, modest, and fairly traditional dress, or blouse and skirt, with sweater and pumps. That's a good start. It's an appropriate ensemble for the venue, whether it be a residence, restaurant, or country club. You've dressed to be considerate of your boyfriend, who's nervous as a long-tailed cat in a room full of rocking chairs. You're also conveying respect to his parents, who may become members of your family in the future. And you've dressed to communicate that you respect yourself. You feel good about yourself. The potential in-laws are impressed. And your boyfriend is appreciative. Easy rule: say to yourself, "If the situation were reversed, how would I like someone to dress or behave for me?"

The Evening Out might be dinner at a restaurant, cocktails on the town, or an elegant dinner party at a residence. This calls for the Simple Black Dress. Simple does not mean dowdy or boring. The dress should flatter you. If well-made and well-tailored, it will serve you well for years and never go out of style. Not too low cut in front, and not too short in length, please. Accessories may include a cozy shawl, colorful scarf, classic clutch, grandmother's pearls, or a single great piece of jewelry.

Why is it important to dress well? Because you want your appearance to make a positive contribution to your image, not be a negative or a distraction. You want to give people a fair chance to get to know you for who you are (social situations), or what you can contribute (work situations), from a neutral or preferably positive starting point. Dressing tastefully is also a reflection of what is going on inside you. It communicates what you think of yourself.

Your appearance should visually communicate that you respect yourself, and that you require other people to respect you, first and foremost, before they make any other judgments about you. This is especially true with a first impression. You have to make dressing well (not necessarily dressing up) a habit.

Caveat: if you are a musician, artist, or writer, or working in the fashion industry, I am completely wasting my breath/ink/paper here. You will dress to express yourself (artist), or barely dress because you genuinely couldn't care less (writer or musician), or dress to impress (fashion). When you enter the entertainment aspect of any of these careers, you will sometimes dress in order to communicate an image and promote your brand. This is called *wardrobe*. It's clothing for a performance. Remember that you need to live a real life, too, and dress for that as well.

Bottom Line: if you want to show respect to the people you care about or an important event, know what the occasion is and dress appropriately.

Old Money Quote: "Dress shabbily and they remember the dress; dress impeccably and they remember the woman."
- Coco Chanel

Things to Remember

If you feel you need guidance to develop a style or a look, I suggest you start with research, then take time to think and consider, then move slowly into purchases. Avoid advertising, fashion blogs, and fashion magazines. Avoid "best-dressed" lists, as they're usually composed of celebrities who have stylists to dress them and publicists to promote them. As discussed, very few buy their own clothes or have a real style of their own.

Instead, research online photos of Jacqueline Kennedy Onassis, Michelle Obama, Christiane Amanpour, Amal Clooney, Katherine Hepburn, Audrey Hepburn, Sophia Loren, and Princess Diana. These women are often referred to as "style icons" because most of the time they have dressed in a classic, refined manner that transcends the eras in which they lived. Each of them expresses their own individual style, regardless of the occasion. As you look at their photos, you'll quickly be able to discern which ensembles they wore that remain timeless. You want to focus on the timeless outfits and implement that style, if not the actual garments, into your wardrobe. Since women come in different sizes and shapes, I encourage you to look for the icon with your body type and analyze how they made the most of their looks.

For the Old Money Gal, the watchwords of style are *simplicity* and *elegance*, in that order. Less really is more. You wear the clothes. They should not wear you. Function and comfort are part and parcel to your wardrobe today. Clothes must fit and wear well. They must last for years, not just for this fashion season. They must be appropriate for the life you are living on a daily basis. They must not be likely to go out of style.

Oscar Wilde once said that fashion is something so bad it has to be changed every six months. Listen to Mr. Wilde. Avoid fashion like the plague. Do research and develop your style. Keep it simple. Keep it traditional. Keep it elegant. When in doubt, lean toward the conservative. Less is more. Less is more. Less is more.

> Note: Old Money Gals regard their clothes as *investments.* With that in mind, you might consider a 5% monthly "set aside" from your net pay to invest in your wardrobe as good values on classic pieces become available. This is not for impulse shopping: this is for deliberate, strategic investing in pieces

that will last decades: a slow approach to building a classic wardrobe. Watch for end-of-season sales. Don't feel compelled to purchase something every month. Keep your wardrobe "set aside" money separate from your regular savings and investment funds. Be patient. *Invest* wisely. Look fabulous.

The Exemplar: Coco Chanel

Coco Chanel is the founder and namesake of the iconic Chanel fashion brand. She's also acknowledged to be the first *influencer* in women's fashion, as well as the first person to take a selfie.

Glamorous as her later life appeared to the public, it didn't start out that way. After her mother's death, young Gabrielle was sent to an orphanage. Life for children there was harsh and accommodations spartan. It was, however, where she would learn to sew, a skill that would change her life, as well as the world of fashion.

Success came early after she constructed a dress from an oversized jersey sweater. When asked about where she got the dress by several people, being a savvy businesswoman, she capitalized on the opportunity and offered to make dresses for them. The cut was stylish, the color choice was bold for that time, associated only with periods of mourning. But Mademoiselle Chanel had a vision, and the "little black dress" was born.

Declaring that, "Luxury must be comfortable, otherwise it is not luxury," she liberated women from the constraints of the "corseted silhouette" and introduced a sporty, casual chic as the feminine standard of style immediately after World War I. This clean, classic, and comfortable style of dress that has endured for almost a century made her famous around the world, and very rich. Still, she wasn't satisfied.

In the 1920s, Coco Chanel, as she was then known, launched her first perfume, Chanel No. 5, the first to feature a designer's name. Perfume "is the unseen, unforgettable, ultimate accessory of fashion. . . . that heralds your arrival and prolongs your departure," she once explained.

A prolific fashion creator, Mademoiselle Chanel extended her influence beyond couture clothing, expanding her design aesthetic to include jewelry and accessories, many marked with her famed interlocked-CC monogram.

The Depression of the 1930s and the outbreak of World War II forced her to close her once-thriving business. Rumors of her romantic involvement with a Nazi military officer during the occupation badly damaged her reputation. While never formally charged with collaborating, the charges nevertheless resonated with French citizens. She was convicted in the court of public opinion and went into self-imposed exile in Switzerland. But she was not finished.

At age 73 she made a triumphant return to the world of fashion with a line of timeless designs that wowed the public, even if they were initially panned by the critics. She worked relentlessly until her death in Paris at age 87.

If you love fashion and think you might want a career in the field, or if you want to "start over" at any age, read more about the life of Coco Chanel.

"I don't do fashion. I am fashion." - Coco Chanel

Best in Class

I call it Old Money Style. It's often called "preppy," sometimes "Ivy Style," referring to the Ivy League schools in the northeast region of the United States, where this mode of dressing originated almost a century ago. Whatever you call it, it's the way Old Money Gals have been dressing for decades.

This traditional, comfortable, discreet, and elegant manner of dress has endured, oblivious to the winds of fashion. It remains a benchmark. Use it as your North Star, should you find yourself at a loss for wardrobe direction. It exclusively involves natural fabrics, leans toward solid colors, and will serve you extremely well over the course of your life.

Should you adopt this style, people may not notice what you're wearing on a specific day, but they will over time come to consider you as always "well dressed," regardless of whether they see you in the office, around the neighborhood, or at a social event.

Again: the way you dress is nonverbal communication. When you opt to dress as an Old Money Gal, your style is communicating some important ideas to others about you: you're confident about your future, secure enough not to have to attract attention strictly with your clothes, independent in your thinking, and unapologetic about your values. You convey the idea that your attributes go much deeper than what meets the eye, and that, in order to find out what those are, someone will have to take an interest and make an effort to get to know you. You're not on display for anyone's amusement, entertainment, or approval.

Furthermore, you establish yourself as a person uninfluenced by passing trends, someone who doesn't need the latest fashion to prop up her self-esteem. You're presenting yourself as someone with self-respect and traditional values—the opposite of arm candy. All these things are going to work in your favor as you make a first impression, and as you create an appearance that conveys how you expect to be treated: fairly and with respect.

Random thing to consider: you've seen family photos that are ten, twenty, or thirty years old. Fashions captured in these images can be ghastly and comical. That's because they are fashions. They are not style. You know who doesn't look silly? Old Money Gals. Because they dress in the same style for decades, from generation to generation, from cradle to grave.

~ *Old Money Secret* ~

How a woman presents herself to the world will determine to a large extent how she is treated by the world and what results she gets from the world. Presentation includes preparation, comportment and manners, and clothing and grooming.

◊ ◊ ◊ ◊

The Short List

If you are a college student, or just starting out in your career, you want to keep your style simple, economical, and classic. Here's a Short List of the basics you can acquire in order to present yourself stylishly for decades:

1. White or sky blue long sleeve, 100% cotton and linen blouses;

2. Solid color 100% cotton short sleeve pullovers;

3. Solid color pullover or cardigan sweaters, 100% wool or 100% cotton;

4. 100% linen or cotton long pants and shorts in solid colors;

5. Grey, black, or navy 100% linen or wool/cashmere blend pants;

6. Grey, black, or navy 100% linen or 100% wool skirts;

7. A classic black dress, mid-length;

8. Black high heel shoes with a closed toe, for office or dress;

9. Navy or tan pumps with a chunk heel, for walking comfortably;

10. Topsiders, sandals, or loafers, for casual;

11. Wool socks and cotton socks and hose, neutral, blue or black;

12. Blue or black blazer;

THE OLD MONEY BOOK

13. Blue, black, or grey business suit of good quality;

14. Navy, grey, or camel tan full-length 100% wool coat for winter;

15. A "London Fog" style trench coat for rain.

Ralph Lauren Polo, Brooks Brothers, L.L. Bean, and Lands' End offer these items in a predictable range of quality and styles, and a wide variety of price points. Remember the Old Money Order of Things: *Plan*...well in advance. *Earn*...like a man. *Save*...consistently. *Invest*...strategically. *Spend*...wisely. *Plan. Earn. Save. Invest. Spend.*

As you strategize to create or recreate your wardrobe, remember: you are *investing* in yourself. Invest in quality products in traditional styles because they stand the test of time. Keep these helpful hints in mind:

- Take your time; let your style develop;

- Remember and follow the "5% set aside" rule;

- Avoid logos, or keep them small and to a minimum;

- Prioritize your purchasing: acquire items you will wear every day first;

- Know that in terms of quality/price, most of the time you will get what you pay for;

- Look for items that wear well over time, both in terms of style and durability;

- Shop at upscale vintage stores for great deals on high-quality, well-maintained, classic garments.

The Real Thing

A stunning, tasteful, original piece of jewelry is an accessory that enhances a woman's natural beauty. Old Money Gals know that, and keep jewelry to a minimum. Follow their lead: keep the bling to a minimum. Make sure it is appropriate. A little goes a long way. Curate great pieces made with quality materials. Know that counterfeit jewelry or accessories are obvious to the refined eye and should be avoided. I feel very strongly about this for two reasons.

First, counterfeiting name brands is a criminal enterprise. It is lucrative. It is global. It is violent. And it victimizes not just the women who buy the fake items, but also the often abused women who work in hellish conditions for slave wages to produce the merchandise. So, considering this, you can decide if you want to participate in this blood-stained economy in order to impress the easily impressed.

Second, I will tell you that Old Money Gals have razor-sharp radar: they can spot a fake Louis Vuitton bag from across the street. Furthermore, Old Money Gals view the display of counterfeit merchandise as a desperate attempt to impress and as a willingness to deceive. Neither of these is appealing. Neither is tolerated. So, do not come crying to me when you have been dissed and dismissed for owning a piece of counterfeit merchandise.

In the words of the classic Motown hit...ain't nothing like the real thing, baby. An authentic Cartier Tank watch or stainless steel Rolex says much more than a gaudy display of diamonds or cubic zirconium. Again: purchase genuine, quality pieces slowly over time. (Unlike counterfeits, they are a wise investment and will last a lifetime.) Extravagant rings, necklaces, and watches have their place. Still, even the most affluent women on the planet opt for discreet luxury when it comes to jewelry to wear on a daily basis.

◊ ◊ ◊ ◊

Ignore the loud logos and labels
the masses often choose;
Listen as real wealth whispers...
"Good manners and good shoes."

- Poem from an Anonymous Old Money Gal

◊ ◊ ◊ ◊

Ladies, as important as attire is, it's more important to live your life on your own terms. I've included this poem to provide some inspiration to all of you.

From *The Old Money Book* blog
June 29, 2018

Song of a Pirate Queen

Song of a Pirate Queen

Oh to be a pirate queen
on a ship upon the sea,
with adventures unknown and lands unseen—
Yes, that's the life for me!

With one eye upon the horizon,
and a bounty of treasure below,
I'll chart my own course,
explore new realms,
and decide for myself

when and where I drop anchor or go.

With a bearing quite regal
I'll inquire of a seagull
any wisdom he'd care to bestow;
As the oceans' royal dauphine,
I'll hold court with the dolphins
as they soar and splash to and fro.

With one hand upon my sword
I'll guard my vessel and my heart:
still open to friendship and passion
however they may start.

Yet no man will capture me
without his surrender first;
For as much as I love love,
without my freedom I am cursed.

With royal blood pushing through my veins
and a full wind in my sails,
I'll live a life as rich as diamonds
and have joys as big as whales.

Who knows what storms may toss me
or in which battle I may fall?

But I'd rather be thrown into the raging deep
than wither in some sleepy port of call.

So as I test my mettle and own my faults—
who knows who or what I'll be?
but first I'll be a Pirate Queen—
Yes, that's the life for me!

◊ ◊ ◊ ◊

Gentlemen, I've provided this small excerpt from *Old Money Style* to introduce a couple of rarely-discussed "thought processes" behind the idea of dressing well on a daily basis. If you're already inclined to dress well, these ideas may help you focus your efforts. If you aren't that interested in dressing well, these two concepts—"The Philosophy Behind Your Wardrobe" and "The Purpose of Your Wardrobe"—may encourage you to upgrade your look.

Either way, here they are...

The Philosophy Behind Your Wardrobe

Why talk about a philosophy of dressing well?

The answer is simple: if we understand *why* something is the way it is, or does what it does, it's easier to digest it, personalize it, and implement it.

Functionally, clothing protects us from the elements—rain, cold, the blazing sun, mosquitos—and keeps us from getting arrested for indecent exposure.

Everything else clothing does, from that basic task forward, is psychological. Remember that.

We use clothing to express ourselves, to communicate, to provoke, and possibly to control or influence the behavior of others, or even ourselves.

Our choice of clothing impacts our daily experiences. For example:

- You may wear a jacket to support your local sports team, identifying and bonding with your "tribe";

- You may be required by your company or boss to dress a certain way in order to appear professional in the workplace for the benefit of your clients and colleagues;

- You may have noticed that children behave better when they're dressed up (ask any teacher on class photo day);

- You may get better service at restaurants and shops when you dress well; and

- You may even feel better about yourself when you dress well.

William Shakespeare, the greatest playwright in history, said, "Clothes maketh the man."

Smart people have known these truths for a long time.

The Uniform

Napoleon Bonaparte, one of the greatest generals of all time, noted that, "A man becomes a creature of his uniform."

So let's talk about a uniform that can work for you.

The "uniform" that we're going to use as a North Star is based on a combination of two sartorial traditions: the prep school uniforms worn by students at private schools in New England, and the no-nonsense style of Old Money Guys living in Boston.

These wardrobe concepts are solid, timeless, and universally effective. We honor these two prototypes because of the values they represent:

- **Education and equality** – every student in a prep school wears the same uniform, and gets the same education, regardless of whether they're rich or poor; and

- **Function and modesty** – season after season, Old Money Guys in Boston wear quality clothes that look good, but don't obviously call attention to their wealth or position in their community.

We also honor them for their simplicity. The prep school student is most often attired in his blue blazer, rep tie, white or blue shirt, with khakis or grey slacks. The Old Money Guy has his go-to tweed jacket, comfortable sweater, dress shirt, warm pants, and sturdy shoes. Nothing fancy. Nothing frilly.

Both the student and the OMG wear what works. They wear what's appropriate for their position and their duties. They don't have to think about it too much. (Admittedly, the prep school student doesn't get to think about their uniform at all: they're just told to put it on and get their ass to class.)

The Process

There is a process I propose you go through in order to create your uniform. I encourage you to take the following steps:

- Learn the importance of quality clothing and what it communicates;

- Prioritize garments you wear daily to make the most of your budget;

- Assemble a balanced inventory of go-to pieces;

- Preserve and protect your investment by organizing, cleaning, and storing your clothes properly;

- Know the outfit that's appropriate for the occasion or the weather;

- Dress each day without worry, confusion, or delay; and

- Get on with life and living.

Remember: in this part of the book, I'm explaining why we dress the way we do and teaching you how to think about clothes. In the second part of this book, we'll explore an itemized inventory with detailed descriptions of those go-to pieces.

This two-step approach will help you build a wardrobe over time that is:

- traditional in style;

- high in quality;

- reasonable in price;

- versatile in use;

- durable in construction; and

- modest in presentation.

All this, without thinking about it too much, but still with an understanding of what you're doing and why.

Now, let's talk about what your wardrobe is supposed to do...

The Purpose of Your Wardrobe

Historically, the purpose of a woman's wardrobe has been to appear desirable. You can discuss and debate among yourselves how much or how little this has changed.

Ideally, the purpose of a man's wardrobe is to appear reliable. Do not think for one second that this has changed. "Can I count on you?" This is one of the great questions in life, central to every human relationship. This is what your partner wants to know. This is what your boss wants to know. This is what your employees want to know. This is what your friends and family want to know.

Present an image of reliability—as someone who honors his commitments, fulfills his responsibilities, and is present emotionally—in the way you dress. Then follow up that presentation with performance—in the way you act.

Dressing to impress is a mistake. Avoid the peacock syndrome: trying to desperately garner attention through flamboyant attire. Avoid the imposter syndrome: trying to appear wealthier than you really are. Anyone you really want to impress can spot a phony a mile away.

Remember the purpose of your wardrobe as you dress for every occasion.

> **Random Rule**: it should take five minutes for someone to realize you are well-dressed. That is how subtle your clothing should be.

When you dress, you are communicating. People will see you, assess you, make an educated guess about your background, conclude that you have certain character traits, assume you have certain abilities, and decide if they want to get to know you before you ever say a word.

All this is determined largely by the style of dress you've adopted. All this happens very quickly, according to psychologists, who estimate this analysis can take about 3 seconds.

Biased? Oh, yes. Likely to continue? Oh, yes.

Lights...Camera...Wardrobe!

Think about this: the same visual process I just described occurs when you're watching a movie. A character enters a scene, and you, the viewer, see him for the first time. If you were experiencing this story as a novel, with written words on the page, the author might take a page and a half to tell you about this character: who is he, where he's from, what he wants, and a description of what he looks like.

A film director doesn't have that much time: the character must be visually communicated to you, the viewer, in seconds.

How does the director do that? She doesn't, actually. A costume designer has been hired do that. The costume designer reads the script, figures out that this character is, let's say, the villain. The designer then finds the right wardrobe for that character so that, when the audience sees the character, they instantly get a good idea of who he is and how he might fit into the film's story.

So when you see John Malkovich enter a scene wearing a warm-up suit, a shiny T-shirt, and a gold chain around his neck, you think, "Oh, there's John Malkovich, I love that guy." Subconsciously, you also think, "In an outfit like that, he's probably the bad guy, because only gangsters wear track suits, silk T-shirts, and gold chains."

In fact, if a guy wears a gold chain in a movie it almost always means he's a gangster. It can be subtle, like the loan shark in *Michael Clayton* who barely had his dangling over his sweater collar, or obvious, like Al Pacino in *Scarface*. But that's the way it is.

Conversely, if you see a movie character wearing a tan corduroy jacket, that character is a journalist. Watch *All the President's Men* with Robert Redford, from the 1970s, or Ewan McGregor in the more recent film *Miles Ahead*, the Miles Davis biopic. Tan corduroy jacket equals journalist.

This process is how visual psychology works. It is important to understand this so that you can use it for your benefit.

People are going to frame your "character" in their mind when they see the way you've dressed. This is your first opportunity to shape their perception and make a good impression.

Of course, whether the speech and action that follow that first impression match their assumptions in terms of character and competence is completely up to you. But the clothing is the starting point that we're addressing here.

◊ ◊ ◊ ◊

As I noted in *Old Money Style*, there are hundreds of books and probably thousands of websites that offer encyclopedic amounts of information on the history and intricacies of men's clothing. We could spend a lifetime and never digest it all.

To fully understand and appreciate some of the more subtle nuances of style, however, may not be found in a book or on a website. You may have to read between the lines, as I recently discovered.

From *The Old Money Book* blog
Feb 10, 2019

Message in a Buckle

The nonverbal communications embedded in French culture are a never-ending source of fascination for me here in Paris. Because I'm not fluent enough in French to catch certain subtle, revealing turns of phrase, I miss that part of the "delivery" that might carry double entendres or hidden gems of humor in conversation.

I do, however, catch a few of the visual clues that Parisians nonchalantly drop to establish their individualism, to communicate status, or otherwise to set themselves apart from the hoi polloi.

Let me set the scene for one example: at a neighborhood café, the regular clientele covers the full spectrum, coming and going at fluid yet routine waves and intervals. Earliest in the morning, standing at the bar, the lime-green clad sanitation workers taking a break from picking up the trash or cleaning the streets.

Coming a few minutes later, and brushing shoulders with them, the suit-clad professionals grabbing a morning cup of ambition (Dolly Parton's phrase, not mine) prior to heading into the office.

A little later, at the bar or at a table near a side door, the local boutique owners complain about the rain and its effects on their businesses, which they'll open in a half hour or so. Then, a half hour later, tourists pack the tables and fuel themselves for a day of sightseeing, their excitement at being in Paris defying the weight of any jet lag.

The footwear of each group is telling: the municipal workers in their clunky and mud-splattered black work boots. The male office workers in their black lace-up dress shoes. The boutique owners in functional dress and casual shoes, often with rubber soles for comfort. The tourists almost always in sneakers.

Sprinkled among these various groups, often in a corner or wedged into a window seat at the end of the counter, is an aging member of the fading French nobility. He may or may not be a (formally, or formerly) titled aristocrat, but there is no doubt of his position in the community.

He has lived here all his life. And by "here" I mean within spitting distance of where he lives now, and most likely in the same residence in which he was born and raised, and in which his ancestors were born and raised, for centuries. His family probably owns several apartments in the immediate area and lives in them, or rents them out, or lets them sit empty, depending on the circumstances and their mood. (They're French and by definition very arbitrary.)

His hair is white or silver. His expression is stoic: if he hasn't seen it all, he's seen a lot. His dress shirt is expensive, but not obviously so. His sweater is cashmere or wool, and has seen its better days, but he doesn't give a damn. His sport coat is tweed, usually an earth tone. He is layered and wrapped like a cashmere and wool turtle in the winter, with at least one scarf cocooning him against the cold. His baggy corduroy pants, often in eye-popping reds and lime greens, are the first class marker: he doesn't dress for the office or for business. He doesn't have a boss. He doesn't have clients who need to approve or think well of him.

In a country where the majority of working men habitually opt for the slim-cut black or navy business suit, white shirt, black or navy tie, and black shoes, these expensive, generous, and colorful cords are the French version of "go-to-hell" pants.

But the most telling sartorial signal is most often left for last as we survey the monsignor from head to toe: the unbuckled monk strap dress shoes. (Less frequent but equally telling is the velvet slipper, usually in black or burgundy.)

The unbuckled shoe sends a couple of important messages to the observant: first, "I didn't walk very far to get here," and "I certainly didn't walk very fast." And, one might add, "I won't be in a hurry whenever I choose to leave." For me, the sound of the jingling buckles conjures an image of an outlaw entering a saloon in an old Western movie, spurs chiming with each step, halting conversation and card-playing by the other patrons.

There's little notice here, in a modern day Parisian café. Tourists are generally oblivious to the local real estate prices (a 1,500 square foot apartment around the corner recently sold for 2.3 million euros). They don't notice the steely, proud bearing of the blue-blooded denizens of our little village. Maybe because the traditional status symbols are absent, well-hidden, or simply fall on deaf ears with many Parisians.

If you're listening, however, the flapping, jingling monk straps softly speak volumes.

DICTION & GRAMMAR

"Speak clearly if you speak at all; carve every word before you let it fall." – Oliver Wendell Holmes, Sr.

Old Money may have a wisp of its regional dialect—a soft Southern drawl or a tight New England clip—but the rough edges have been polished. Old Money generally speaks what is known as Standard American English.

Old Money pronounces its words clearly in a soft to moderate volume. The voice does not have an unpleasant nasal tone or a grating twang. It is not shrill. The vocal chords are not strained because the speech is supported by breath, which originates deep in the lungs and not the throat. The pace of speech is not so rapid it cannot be understood; it is not so slow that the listener loses interest before a sentence is finished.

Regarding grammar, when someone asks, "How are you?" Old Money will reply, "I'm well, thank you." Others will reply, "I'm good, thank you." Good, as opposed to bad? Or good...at what?

Old Money is articulate. It has a large vocabulary and uses the right word to convey the right idea. Old Money constantly increases its vocabulary by learning new words. If you feel your vocabulary could improve (and all of ours could), make it a habit to learn the meaning and pronunciation of one new word each day. When you read a book or article and come across a word you're unfamiliar with, make a note of the word and research its meaning. Then go back and see in what context it was used.

Old Money does not use its vocabulary as a way to intimidate or exclude others, or to show how educated or sophisticated it is. While Old Money is never rude, it does not verbally dress up a situation to make it seem better than it is. Old Money can be blunt and concise, but its thinking is sharp, detailed, and circumspect. And that shows in its vocabulary.

Note: when you begin to change your speech patterns with an eye to self-improvement, you will be more inclined to speak properly when you are around your business colleagues or others of a higher social standing. You may then revert back to slang, lazy grammar, or colloquialisms when you are simply "hanging out with friends." Beware: this will not serve you well. When you work to change, make the change slow, permanent, and comprehensive. Otherwise, you may be seen as a phony who only behaves a certain way around a certain group of people. It may also cause inner conflict, as you may feel you do not know who you really are.

For Reference

Speak Up by Sam Chwat is an excellent resource for eliminating regional accents and learning to speak Standard American English.

The Best Little Grammar Book Ever by Arlene Miller is an excellent resource for correcting common mistakes in grammar.

Numerous sources for speech and grammar improvement exist online and at your local public library.

The Relationship

For the serious, or those who speak publicly or to groups often, seek out a professional speech therapist. Their rates are often very reasonable. The techniques they teach in a few weeks can benefit for a lifetime.

DICTION & GRAMMAR
That Was Then. This Is Now.

I'd like to tell you that grammar and diction have improved immensely since I first published this book in 2013. They have not. I hear mispronounced words spoken by native English speakers regularly on television. When you make a request of someone, you "ask" them to do something. You do not "axe" them to do something. You are not "fixing to do" something in the future, my dear Texans. You are going to do it at some point in the future.

Words are not only mispronounced; they are misused. I read headlines in well-respected newspapers that proclaim something is "wrong" when in actuality it is *inaccurate* or *untrue*. The Ford Motor Company presented car commercials which encouraged potential buyers to "Go Further," which would mean to go into more detail. I think an automobile company would want us to "Go Farther," which refers to physical distance.

Why am I so obsessed with the proper use of the spoken and written language? Because it is essential for us to communicate exactly what we mean. It is important in our personal relationships when we want to express our feelings. It is vital in our business communications so that our customers and colleagues have a clear understanding of what service we intend to provide or what goods we intend to purchase. It is vital for democracy, too. We must watch for the euphemisms that clever candidates and slippery public officials use when they put some polish on a bad policy, or marginalize a sector of our society.

More importantly, we must monitor our own patterns of speech and make sure bad habits don't creep in. One common tendency for Americans is to use the word *like* too often and incorrectly. "And I was like, you know, getting really angry, and she was all like, hey, don't be mad with me, and we were like, yelling at each other..." And I can like, listen to someone speak like this for about, you know, like a minute before I'm ready to like, scream. I'm not alone in my concerns for the proper use of words.

In 1635, the French established the Academie Francaise, which attempts to preserve and protect the French language. The council still arbitrates on all matters linguistic, reflecting the very French habit of precision: using exactly the right word to communicate the specific idea. The government of Iceland is also vigilant. They will not allow certain foreign words to appear in their dictionary out of concerns for their language. Very few people in the world speak it, and they want to maintain its purity.

As English speakers, we have the luxury of being the language of the digital age. We also have a history of welcoming new words into our vocabulary. Still, we need to elevate our standards. Good grammar is critical. Proper diction speaks volumes.

We need to say exactly what we mean, even if it means pausing during the drafting of an email or during a casual conversation, to find the right word to do so.

And, of course, we also need to mean what we say, but that's another issue.

FURNISHINGS

"See that coffee table? It's two hundred years old. Put your feet on it. Put your drink on it. We don't care. We use our things. Just don't get so drunk you fall and break it. Mother would go nuts." – OMG in Connecticut

Old Money has the benefit of inheriting sofas, chairs, tables, and the like from well-heeled ancestors who had an eye for quality, the means to acquire it, and the brains to hold on to it. Perhaps you've inherited good pieces, and you've been spared the expense of furnishing your residence from scratch.

If not, fret not. There is hope. And that hope lies in the ignorance, negligence, and poor judgment of others. Can't we always count on that? These "others" are the people whose families have acquired quality furnishings in the past, but no living member of the family has the inclination, interest, or intelligence to hold on to them. Therefore, these quality pieces end up at auctions, thrift shops, garage sales, and estate sales at a fraction of their value. Not very Old Money, but good for you (wink, nod).

This, like many endeavors of Old Money, takes time, patience, and cash. But with these, and a little luck, in a relatively short period of time, a young man, woman, or couple can start with a vacant apartment and end up with a well-furnished abode full of sturdy, comfortable and attractive sofas, tables, lamps and chairs.

The first thing to know is where to go. Trendy vintage and antique stores are fine, but they have overhead and are in business to make money. Therefore, the prices may be higher. Thrift stores run by charities and garage sales in your neighborhood are better bets. The overhead at these venues is less and the priority is more likely to be getting the furniture out of the store or the garage rather than making a tidy profit. The same can be said for items listed on websites like Craigslist.

A very good source for quality furnishings is your local auction house. High-end auction houses like Sotheby's and Christie's sell art and antiques. Prices can run into the millions of dollars. Old Money can, and often does, buy there. But if you're just starting out or starting over, auction houses liquidating the contents of local estates for heirs or creditors are a great place to get sofas, chairs, rugs, and tables for a fraction of their retail price. These items are generally traditional in style, sturdy in construction, and vary considerably in condition. They can be like new, or they can be worn threadbare.

In any case, the items available at these auctions—where items sell for a dollar to ten thousand dollars—are great potential values. Again, they do require patience, forethought, and cash, but the savings are worth it. The auctions are also great fun.

The most important thing to do prior to attending the actual auction is to preview the items up for sale. The preview happens either a few days or a few hours before the auction. This provides the shrewd buyer the chance to browse all the items for sale, closely inspect any items of interest, and review the auction house catalogue to get an idea of auction estimates for each piece.

A sofa that looks great from a few feet away may have structural issues that are only visible upon closer inspection. A chair that looks awful from a distance might have hand-carved legs that are sturdy and beautiful. The preview provides an opportunity to assess the merchandise and the other buyers. These buyers may not be dressed like the society matrons at Sotheby's but they have money. They are often the proprietors of the antique and vintage retail stores you decided not to frequent. They will bid on quality merchandise here at the auction, acquire it at sometimes a ridiculously low price, and then put it on the showroom floor across town at a hefty markup. This retail price will be paid by someone with more money than sense, but that's business. It's just not the way Old Money does business.

After the preview, but prior to the auction, you'll have the chance to look at the auction house catalogue. You'll probably note several items you want to bid on (remember, you're still buying things you're going to use every day). You'll look at the auction estimates and eliminate items that most likely will not be in your budget. But don't rule any of them out completely; there are surprises at every auction. Some items sell for many times their estimate; some sell for next to nothing, regardless of their estimate. Watch for opportunities as the items you like come up for sale.

When the bidding starts on an item you're interested in, remain calm. Do not bid first. Do not bid quickly. Take the temperature of the room. Is there a lot of interest? Or almost none? Bid strategically. Know your budget. Do not get carried away. There will be another chair or another table another day. Also be aware that there will be a 10% premium added to the item you buy, plus sales tax. That can increase the cost of your new treasure 20% over and above the sale price. And if it's a large sofa or table, you still have to get it from the auction house to your house. So a $50 armchair might end up costing $100 by the time it finally comes to rest in your living room.

Nevertheless, the bargains found at these auction houses are almost always amazing. Note, too, that auctions are social events. People meet, talk, bid against each other, and have fun in between bidding. But be polite; don't talk while bidding is in progress.

Auction houses are great places to find furniture, dishes, glassware, and table linens. Just make sure to preview any item you plan to bid on.

When you're looking at a piece of furniture, whether you're at a garage sale, thrift store, or auction house, the thing to do is ignore the fabric and look at the frame. At first glance, a green- and yellow-checked sofa from the 1970s might be a ghastly thought. But if you can see past that, and find hand-carved wood and a set of springs that are still solid, you may be onto something. Imagine what the sofa would look like in a tan-colored velvet, or with a couple of pillows. Sofas and armchairs are often found for pennies—compared with buying new things retail. And Old Money never pays retail for new furniture. If Old Money does pay a premium for a piece of furniture, it is an antique that will hold its value, appreciate over time, and can be sold by an auction house—like Sotheby's or Christie's—for a good price.

Once you have acquired a sofa or set of chairs, you may want to have them reupholstered to suit your tastes. Take your time. Find a fabric store in your area and select enough fabric to cover the furniture, and perhaps a little extra to have pillows made. They have illustrated charts for guidance. Nothing too splashy, flashy, or trashy. Elegant, timeless, durable, comfortable. You want anyone, from the President of the United States to the local butcher, to be able to come into your home and feel at home. You're not creating a showroom. You're creating a place in which to live on a daily basis. Refer to hardcover books that show pictures of Old Money residences rather than contemporary home decorating magazines that cater to the middle class and nouveau riche.

If you're just starting out, or starting over, earth tone fabrics will serve you well. Splashes of bright colors on pillows and accessories add life and are easily interchangeable.

Ask friends, relatives, and colleagues for a referral to a local upholstery shop. This shop is almost always owned by an older gentleman. Look at his work. If you like it, discuss price. You may have options: he can provide the fabric, if he has a good selection, or you may find the fabric yourself and provide it to him. Weigh these and decide. He will pick your furniture up, reupholster it in a week or two, then deliver it. The cost to acquire quality furniture second-hand and have it reupholstered is far less than paying retail for it. Plus, you get exactly what you want. It may take longer, but it lasts longer. Many Old Money households never buy new furniture; they simply have their existing pieces reupholstered every ten or twenty years, if at all.

Note: if you acquire your furniture one piece at a time, it may have a mismatched look until you get it reupholstered (and perhaps even afterward). This is understandable, and not entirely unwelcome. If it bothers you, paint the walls of the room in question a very bright color. This will draw the eye away from the furniture and give an otherwise traditional room a lively kick.

But be cautious: splash a sample color on a white wall and leave it for a week or two to see how it settles with your eye and your décor. "It seemed like a good idea at the time" is not something you want to say to yourself after you've painted an entire room.

Remember: don't waste money on buying new furniture for retail. This rule can also apply to dishes, table linens, and rugs. Goodwill stores and off-the-beaten-path resale shops are gold mines for finding quality furnishings at bargain prices.

Note: Old Money doesn't live with white walls. They're too stark. Paint can soften a room's atmosphere and encourage relaxation, or stimulate it (like red for a dining room) and contribute to appetite and conversation. Use it.

Feng Shui is the ancient art of creating harmony in your living and working space. While many scoff at it, many Old Money Chinese adhere to its principles and prosper. Consider learning about it and applying the fundamentals of the practice to your home and office.

Online resources are your first stop in order to familiarize yourself with the concepts of this tradition. A book is second. Acquiring the services of a Feng Shui Master to address the issues of your home or office is third.

Helpful Hints

- If you have children or plan to have children, rethink the white satin sofa fabric.

- Area rugs on hardwood floors are preferable to carpet.

- We've all seen the framed print of the dogs playing cards. Don't.

- Used pianos sell for about one quarter the price of an identical new piano. Check the classifieds when the children are ready for lessons.

- For inexpensive and interesting wall décor, display your hobby: use secondhand picture frames and frame the wine labels from vintages you've enjoyed, maps of countries or cities you love, or sepia-tint photos of a family pet. They're easy, and personal.

- Plants not only make a room more attractive, they oxygenate it as well. Make room for a few in each room.

- Water them. Talk to them. Play classical music to help them grow (we are not joking).

- If you share a house with a spouse, do not dominate a common room with your decorative tastes alone.

- Gentlemen, keep the black leather chairs and vintage calendars in the designated man cave. Ladies, go easy on the frilly accessories.

- Moderate the size and number of electronics in the house. One television and one stereo system are enough. Lean toward books, plants, and a décor that encourages conversation and reflection.

For Reference

Feng Shui Your Life by Jayme Barrett offers a comprehensive and accessible guide to making the most of this ancient science.

The Relationship

A local craftsman who reupholsters furniture at reasonable prices.

A paint brush, which you will use yourself to paint the walls.

A Feng Shui master to bring harmony to your living space.

FURNISHINGS
That Was Then. This Is Now.

Current economic conditions may dictate that you live in a small space, or at least something smaller than what you'd like. If that's the case, look at the situation less as a limitation and more as an opportunity to refine your interior design and organizational skills.

Consider the following in order to maximize the space you call home:

- A vintage steamer trunk that can be used as a coffee table to take advantage of the storage space inside it.

- A sofa that has built-in storage in the arms and perhaps folds out into a bed.

- A "secretary," i.e., a piece of furniture that serves as a writing desk and storage cabinet. This piece of furniture is usually very traditional in style, moderate to small in size, and versatile in use.

- A drop-leaf table that can accommodate four to six people for a meal, then fold up to fit snugly against a wall.

- Folding screens or curtains that can temporarily divide a room for privacy, then fold up to take up little space in a corner after use.

- A large, full-length framed mirror to bounce the light and create the feeling of a larger space. These are great in a bedroom, and they don't have to be hung on the wall. They can just sit on the floor and lean against the wall.

One of the most underused spaces in your residence is often underneath and around your bed. Furniture designers offer numerous options to make great use of this area. Some options include:

- A bed with a lift-up mattress that springs up and open to reveal storage beneath the mattress.

- A bed with built-in drawers or shelves in the space underneath the frame.

- A bed with storage space built into the headboard and/or footboard.

- A bed with a raised frame to allow for your own boxes or containers to fit underneath.

- A Murphy bed that folds up and disappears into a wall cabinet.

For more ideas and inspiration, discover how limited space has been maximized in luxury pleasure boats, customized motor homes, container/modular homes, trailers, and tiny houses.

Locate online and print publications that cover each of these industries. You'll find photos and design concepts that will help you make better use of the space you have now...and the space you might be moving into in the future.

READING

"Show me a family of readers, and I will show you the people who move the world." – Napoleon Bonaparte

Old Money reads. It's that simple.

Reading is probably the most important mental exercise you can do. It is vitally important that you do it on a regular basis. It is weight lifting for your brain, and the muscles you are building when you read are *learning ability* and *memory*. This is not your Aunt Edna speaking. This is neuroscience.

If you have not been fortunate enough to have received a top-shelf formal education, you can compensate for that by adopting a joyful and enriching curriculum of your own making. If you have received a quality formal education, do not let your soul atrophy. Build on your strong foundation.

Reading will improve the quality of your life and the quality of your relationships, as the quality of your conversation will in large part be dependent on what you have read. Intelligent, well-read people seldom have lengthy or regular conversations with those who have not read well.

A good regimen for reading is to alternate: read a book that you want to read about a subject that interests you, a guilty pleasure, even. Then read a book that you should read, a classic. Read novels, and you'll discover how history repeats itself and how people really don't change. Read poetry, and you'll discover that the words of love and pain have a surprising timelessness about them. Read philosophy, and you'll discover whether you have one or not. Read plays. If you read Shakespeare, it may help to read it out loud. Don't be embarrassed. You won't be the first to do it and enjoy it.

Biographies of great men and women will offer a glimpse of the very human person behind the legend. Their stories will inevitably reveal dark moments, which may help when you encounter dark moments of your own. They came through theirs and prevailed. So will you.

The quality of the material you read will either elevate your intellectual abilities or erode them. You are also trading precious time to load ideas into your brain. Select your materials with care.

Make your television time your reading time. Your life and your home will change for the better almost immediately.

If you've only read what's required for school or work, you're living half a life.

If someone mentions a title or an author that sounds interesting, make a note. The person who mentioned it will be flattered. A shared joy is a great relationship starter.

Avoid enormous retail bookstores that sell the latest celebrity confessionals and TV-chef cookbooks. Find resale book shops with knowledgeable staff and passionate owners, and thrift stores that resell books.

Helpful Hints

- The plays of William Shakespeare (or the 17th Earl of Oxford, if you prefer)

- The poems of Walt Whitman

- The short stories of Edgar Allan Poe and Washington Irving

- The novels of Charles Dickens

- The essays of Ralph Waldo Emerson

- The meditations of Marcus Aurelius

- The life of Lord Byron

- The thoughts of Tagore

For Reference

The Western Canon: The Books and School of the Ages by Harold Bloom provides a dazzling overview of great literary works and their authors.

A subscription to an international newspaper is invaluable in gaining a global perspective on current events. Consider *The Guardian*, published in London. Their weekly publication is articulate, comprehensive, and refreshing.

Magazine subscriptions are an economical way to stay entertained and informed, but make sure the publications cover subject matter that is worthy of you. The subject matter contained in publications that you read and browse through repeatedly may shape your priorities and influence your decision-making process, especially with regards to the advertising contained within. They can numb your mind or elevate your thinking, so take care in choosing your subscriptions.

The Relationship

Your local public library and your librarian.

Family, friends, and colleagues who read. Ask them what they're reading. Find a subject of interest. Dive in.

READING
That Was Then. This Is Now.

The roster of great authors and their works never really changes, it only expands. Please allow me to include Jane Austen, Mary Shelley, Emily Dickinson, the Bronte sisters, Agatha Christie, Harper Lee, Louisa Mae Alcott, Alice Walker, Maya Angelou and Edith Wharton in the list.

One of the things I've come to enjoy is not simply reading the works of great writers, but reading their biographies as well. I find that I learn how their personal lives and the times in which they lived influenced their works. It adds a dimension of understanding and appreciation.

Enjoy.

◊ ◊ ◊ ◊

Of course, during the confinement here in Paris, there was a lot of time to read. There was a lot of time to do a lot of other things, too, which I addressed in the poem below.

From *The Old Money Book* blog
May 14, 2020

All The Things I'd Planned To Do

I had a moment—well, more than a few—
to look back on all the things I'd planned to do.
Oh, the itinerary was going to be insane:
London by rail, Cannes by plane.

But then disease arrived, escorted by dread,
and laid the best-laid plans to rest instead.
Now as the weeks have passed,
I have, at last,
calculated a small but thoughtful sum
of all the things I've actually done.

I've reached back out to friends I'd known
whose once well-worn paths had become overgrown,
and sat for a quiet, nostalgic moment on the phone,
and talked and laughed and listened.

I paused and let an empty space
of quiet contemplation grace
the once busy bustle of work's daily pace
and let silence take its rightful place
as dawn approached and warmed and glistened.

I gave a careful and considered review
of all the things I thought I had to do:
once so important and now so small,
if not accomplished...oh, the sky would fall!
But it did not, I'm now aware.
And going forward, I thought, chin resting in my hand,
After this, what then? What was The Plan?

The future, once so certain-seeming
wondered like a child, day-dreaming.
And did not answer, or even care.

For we are not the mighty gods we think
who conquer and boast and toast and drink;
we are but lost and passing ghosts
who prosper or perish at the pleasure of our Host,
and as triumph and disaster around us dance
we pretend to control what is more often chance,
as we seldom if ever seem to get around to
all the things we'd planned to do.

HOUSING

"Where thou art, that is home." – Emily Dickinson

The first thing Old Money looks for in a residence is safety. Is the neighborhood safe? Is the building safe? Are the water and gas sources and systems safe? The second thing Old Money requires is that the dwelling be affordable. Is the monthly expense for the place—rent, utilities, and any associated fees—within the budget? The third thing Old Money requires is cleanliness. This means keeping the living space and its surroundings clutter-free and hygienic. The fourth thing Old Money considers is the neighborhood. Are schools a factor? Is transportation convenient? How long is the commute to work? What businesses and services are in the area? Is a park, museum, or library nearby?

Emotions are not a part of this decision-making process. Plush carpeting, modern appliances in the kitchen, a great view, or a swimming pool for tenants means nothing. Functionality and affordability are the key elements when Old Money selects a residence.

If you are just starting out or starting over, feel free to rent rather than rush into owning a primary residence. OMGs seek financial independence first, if they do not already have it, and then seek the comfort of owning a primary residence later.

Old Money lives far below its means, especially with regards to housing, because home ownership or rent can be the largest expense in the household budget.

Old Money chooses the neighborhood first and the house second. Better to live in a smaller residence in a better neighborhood than a bigger residence in a lesser neighborhood.

Old Money will make sure good schools, public or private, are available in the neighborhood. The children's education comes first. Old Money, if necessary, will relocate in order to ensure a quality education for the children.

Old Money has a small percentage of its overall net worth invested in a primary residence because a primary residence is very often an expense and not an income-producing asset. Members of the middle class will save and borrow in order to purchase a primary residence which will do nothing but require further expenditures to maintain. The mortgage will also be the largest monthly expense of the household. Opportunities for career advancement, savings, or investment may be missed if the mortgage is too large or consumes too much of the household budget.

The middle class wants to buy a house as soon as possible. They are generally misguided in their financial thinking. They are sold the idea of a house as something that creates security, comfort, and safety, which it does not. It demands a down payment and creates a serious, long-term obligation and, many times, a huge commitment of resources. The purchase of a residence prior to being financially independent profits the owner of the property and the real estate agent, not the buyer.

Again, this is the case of people trying to solve an emotional issue with a financial decision. Old Money doesn't do this. It solves its emotional problems by objective self-examination and sets them apart from financial decisions.

Old Money, if it does not inherit a home, will rent first, keeping and conservatively investing the money it would have put into a down payment. It will purchase a primary residence later in life, make a larger down payment, have lower monthly payments, and more financial independence. It will then leave the house, with a small or non-existent mortgage and tremendous equity, to its children to live in, rent, or sell, when it's time to downsize.

If you absolutely must buy a piece of real estate when you are just starting out or starting over, consider an income-producing one. A residence with two or four units—one you live in and the others you rent out—can moderate the costs of home ownership and provide tax benefits.

Old Money rarely makes renovations, but if it does, it makes sure that they add value to the property. Many additions and alleged "improvements" do not. Consult a local, trusted realtor before remodeling and spending hard-earned money. Make sure it will pay off in resale value.

Do not take out a second mortgage to do renovations. Pay cash. If you are hesitant about parting with hard-earned cash to make improvements, that should tell you something.

Helpful Hints

- Wear a sweater. Open a window. Light a fire. Turn on a fan. Central air is money.

- Check the insulation.

- Hang heavy curtains in winter.

- Leaky faucets are literally money going down the drain.

- Turn off the light when you leave the room.

- Fewer rooms, larger rooms.

- Smaller house, larger lot, quiet street.

- Less stuff, more room.

HOUSING
That Was Then. This Is Now.

At this point in time (the latter part of 2020), I don't think it's a good idea for anyone to purchase a residential property. However, since I do not give financial or investment advice to individuals or companies, simply consider this my personal opinion in print. I will explain why I think this, and you can weigh the value of my perspectives and make your own decisions.

First and foremost, there is very little job security right now, despite how robust some industries may appear or how confident some pundits may be about our future. I'm optimistic about our future, too, but optimism and mortgage payments are two very different things. Math is not negotiable.

If you are renting right now, with solid employment and three months', six months', or one year's worth of living expenses in cash, in the bank, then you're okay. Stay that way. Handing over a load of cash as a down payment and then taking on the responsibilities of mortgage payments, maintenance costs, and property taxes is a big move in a very uncertain time.

Remember: big moves in uncertain times are best when they're business moves that offer the possibility for big profits, not home-buying moves that offer the certainty of greater expenditures.

Also, know the public policy environment you're in right now and be aware of its natural tendencies. As jobs are lost and businesses close, tax revenues also decline. Municipal authorities are going to be hard-pressed for cash. Many will, as they historically do, turn to property tax increases to make up the shortfall. If you become a homeowner, they will look to you and your real estate as a revenue source. If you remain a tenant, your landlord may respond to this property tax increase and raise your rent. Still, that increase will be pennies on the dollar compared to what owners of single-family homes may face in the coming months and years.

Furthermore, as the economy falters, so do banks. Banks supply credit to businesses, and businesses provide jobs to people who make mortgage payments to banks. It's a lovely merry-go-round until the music stops. When that happens, foreclosures become commonplace, property values drop, and consumers—not banks—pay a dear price, one way or another.

Know this: rent is not always "throwing your money away each month," as many will tell you. It may be a strategy to keep your overhead low and your cash reserves healthy during this tricky period. Note: some people will tell you that paying interest to a bank for decades might be "throwing your money away each month," as well.

You also have to consider how fluid and mobile your life is right now if you're renting (or living at home with your parents or another family member). If you do not own a home, and you get a great job offer on the other side of the country, you accept the offer, pack your stuff in boxes, rent a U-Haul truck, and hit the open road.

If you own a traditional, single-family home, you have much more to contend with. You must find a real estate agent you trust, list your home for sale, get it ready to show, make repairs a potential buyer may want to have done, wait for an offer, close the sale, find a new place in a new city, and probably look at buying all over again.

What's more, many young people face the harsh, unfair reality that their student loan debt is their mortgage for the time being. Government action on this front will hopefully be forthcoming, but until it is, we must face things as they are.

Again, the strategy for surviving and thriving in this reality is:

- low monthly overhead;

- consistent savings and/or debt reduction;

- prudent investments (including investments in yourself, such as education); and

- **no screw-ups**.

If I need to explain, screw-ups include criminal behavior in general, drug and alcohol abuse in particular, hasty marriages, and unplanned pregnancies. Toss in gambling and spending addictions just to round out the roster, and you have a fairly good list of what not to do during this or any other time.

If you are living at home with your parents or a family member right now, by choice or by necessity, I know it can be challenging to say the least. To handle the situation best, know why you're doing it. Have a savings plan so you can see the money stack up each month as you don't pay rent to someone else. Have a larger plan, too. Know what your goals are as far as your career and, you know, life in general. Goals have actions and deadlines attached to them, if you remember, and it's best if you share them with the people you're living with, so they know what you're working toward.

As I've said before, if you still want to buy a piece of real estate right now, consider income property. It is more likely to hold its value or increase in value over time. Why? Because its value isn't what another consumer will pay for it. Its value is what another investor will pay for it, based in large part on how much rental income it produces each month. Remember that you'll still have a mortgage payment each month, and the rental income may or may not cover that entire amount.

Also, if a tenant loses their job and can't pay the rent, be ready to ask them to leave, cover some or all of the rent for them, or evict them. That's part of being a landlord, and it is definitely part of it during these difficult times.

Regarding single-family home ownership, I know that the idea is appealing, especially when you have children in the picture. But this is a new world, and home ownership may not be the priority right now. Right now, survival is the priority for many people, and remaining financially independent is the priority for many others. Money for your child's education is going to be paramount. Recognize and accept this new reality and, as French parents often advise their children, *"Soyez sage."* Be wise.

If you do purchase a single-family home, one tactic you may consider is doing everything you can to pay off your mortgage as quickly as possible. This will mean foregoing luxuries like vacations and new cars. Instead you'll double up on mortgage payments in order to attack the principal and not have most of your monthly payment allocated to interest. Many families who immigrate to the United States, especially from southeast Asia, have done this when they purchase a home. Every family member works and contributes to the goal of owning the house outright as soon as possible. Many times this is accomplished in five years, sometimes ten, but it is not easy.

However, once the sacrifice is made and the mortgage paid off, the house really belongs to the family and can finally be considered an asset.

Alternatives to traditional brick-and-mortar home ownership have become very popular in the last couple of years. Residential units constructed from shipping containers and other materials are now available to consumers globally, as are the more familiar trailers and RVs (recreational vehicles) which can be quite luxurious.

Attractive aspects of these innovative designs and models include:

- the low price tag (shipping container homes can start at as little as $50,000);

- a lower carbon footprint than traditional, full-sized homes;

- the ability to customize interior and exterior design elements; and

- portability.

One particular type of low-cost, minimal square footage housing is the tiny house. These stand-alone structures often resemble traditional houses in construction and materials, but they usually have less than 400 square feet in living space.

While these relatively new trends in housing may not be options for a married couple with two growing children, they do present options to single adults and couples who want to preserve their cash, minimize their expenses, and live a simpler life.

I know you've heard it a thousand times, but still, hear it again: the world is a different place after this pandemic. What will return to normal and what will be forever changed is unknown. Until the smoke clears (a few years from now), be conservative with how much you commit to housing.

SOCIALIZING

"Most of the people that work for me are probably more intelligent than I am. The one thing that I can do is walk into a room where I don't know anybody and leave knowing five people I could either become friends with or do business with. I don't always like doing it, but I've learned to do it because I like the results." – OMG in Philadelphia

Old Money leads an active and vibrant social life. Old Money celebrates life. You should, too.

Friends, family, classmates, and colleagues comprise the social network of Old Money, as they do for most people. Even in this age of the internet, socializing by Old Money is done primarily face-to-face at casual or formal events specifically designed for social interaction.

Old Money does not habitually socialize in bars, though the occasional after-work drink is not unheard of. Most socializing occurs in private homes, restaurants, or private clubs.

Conversation is the lifeblood of Old Money socializing. Lively, intelligent, interesting conversation is what defines an Old Money social event more than any other quality. The ability to engage in conversation comfortably and enjoyably with people one has never met is a hallmark of Old Money.

For the shy or inexperienced, it simply requires the practice of a few fundamentals.

Know how you're expected to dress and what time you're expected to arrive at an event. Know the reason, if there is one, for the event. When in doubt, OMGs fall back on the blue blazer and the black dress discussed in the "Attire" chapter. Unless specifically told not to, or you are attending a formal event, bring a bouquet of flowers, dessert, or bottle of wine for the host or hostess if the event is at their home. If you are attending a formal event, have flowers delivered to the host the day before or after.

Know if it's permissible to bring a guest before asking someone to accompany you. If the hosts have invited you and not invited you to bring a guest, don't ask to bring one. This may put them in an awkward position, or they may have someone in mind for you to meet. Know someone very, very well before inviting them to accompany you to a social event. You'll be measured by your guest's behavior, as it is a reflection on your taste and judgment.

When meeting someone, shake their hand firmly and smile. Remember their name. Use their name when you address them in initial conversation. This will help you re-member it.

Ask questions. Listen. Look the person in the eye.

Do not ask personal questions such as what someone does for a living, how much money they make, or what kind of car they drive. You may ask them where they are from or how they know the host of the event you are both attending. If you are drinking wine, ask them if they know anything about wine.

Compliment them sincerely on something about their appearance you like. Not their breasts.

When asked a question, respond honestly but diplomat-ically. Elaborate a little, but remember: conversation is an ex-change. One word answers can kill it, but so can monologues.

Don't *try* to be funny. You're either funny or you're not. In either case, use humor cautiously during an initial conversation. Do not tell jokes. Do not do a stand-up comedy routine. You may tell brief—emphasis on *brief*—interesting stories about things you have done or want to do. Immediately after doing so, however, direct the conversation back to the person or persons you're talking with. Ask about their interests.

Note: these stories are infinitely more appealing if they are not boastful and avoid death, destruction, and disease.

Don't monopolize someone's time. Everyone is there to socialize. After a few minutes of conversation, feel free to thank them for talking with you, tell them you enjoyed it, and ask to be excused to get a drink refreshed, use the restroom, or simply say hello to other guests. If you'd like to talk more with them, ask them for a business card or ask if they'd make time to speak more before the event is over.

Old Money social events are upbeat. Conversation is lively and optimistic. Tragedy, personal problems, and unpleasant topics are not discussed.

If you do something stupid or clumsy, and we all do, simply try to minimize the damage, clean it up or correct it, apologize if necessary and say, "That was embarrassing." And then move on. Talk about something else. If you're around Old Money, they'll play it off like it was nothing and join you in changing the subject and try to make everyone feel comfortable again.

"Networking" among Old Money is done very, very diplomatically. When you tell someone what you do or what you are interested in doing for a living, wait for them to inquire further about it. Do not press. Old Money can spot a sales pitch a mile away.

Social Clues You Can Use

- Regardless of how much you really, really feel the music, do not dance if no one else is dancing.

- Do not dance on a table, even if others are dancing.

• Unless you are specifically asked by the host or hostess, do not sing or play a musical instrument, no matter how well you sing or play.

• It's a party. Stay with the group. If you are invited to a secluded part of the house by another guest or the host, politely decline. If you go to a secluded part of the house with another guest or the host during the party, your good reputation may not be there when you return, regardless of what does or does not transpire in private.

• No matter how hot it may be, do not remove your clothing. If other people remove their clothing, you are not at an Old Money social event. Leave before you see something you'll regret.

• Know when to thank your hosts and leave.

• If you came alone, leave alone. If you came with a guest, leave with that guest, unless they are driving and have been drinking. Then inform your host.

• Do not drink and drive. Call a cab. It's cheaper than bail. Cliché, but true.

• Send a thank you note the next day, without fail.

• Old Money socializing is to connect with friends, share experiences, meet new people, and facilitate business relationships. It is not a place to troll for marriage or sex partners.

• Flirting is fine, just keep it between the lines.

- If Old Money encourages you to meet and talk with someone, make every effort to meet and talk with them. There's a reason.

SOCIALIZING
That Was Then. This Is Now.

It's sad that the word *social* is now often followed by the word *distancing*. As you socialize now, you must consider the health risks of each event you think about attending, including the venue, the other participants, and the local infection rates.

You even have to weigh these when you host or attend a dinner party at a private residence. I'll tell you this now: no one has any idea about the duration, severity, or scope of subsequent, secondary health impacts resulting from or related to COVID-19. Too many people are going to get very sick and not recover from this illness. It is unknown how many people are going to have pulmonary, respiratory, or neurological complications that come on late and strong, weeks, months, or years after their initial bout with the virus.

Again, I am not being an alarmist. While the headlines carry more sensational statistics on the millions of infections and hundreds of thousands of deaths worldwide, articles about these complications and repercussions are already making the news.

What impact this will have on health systems and society is unknown, but right now, it certainly affects how you socialize and with whom. You probably won't regret not attending a party. You might regret attending one.

Socialize selectively. Wear a mask.

◊ ◊ ◊ ◊

As polite and diplomatic as we all try to be in daily life, there will be times that require us to speak up and speak out. Knowing when, how, and where to do this is one of the great mysteries in life.

Still, we must do it.

From *The Old Money Book* blog
May 26, 2017

The Statement and The Stand

The writer voiced his opinions,

right and left and loud,

to an eager group of minions,

a young, impressionable crowd.

But back and a little to the side

sat a solitary man,

listening wearily as he eyed

the glass of whiskey in his hand.

The writer went on and they all heard

about his blogs and posts and tweets,

his audience hungry for every word

like children anxious for their sweets.

Finally taking a satisfied pause

the writer looked over past the rest,

basking in their near applause
took issue with this guest.

"Something's on your mind, I see,"
as the soldier looked his way;
"Is it that you don't agree with me
and all I've had to say?"

"Oh, I've heard much of what you've said
and your words certainly sound fine;
they've originated in a quite educated,
cultivated, and sophisticated mind."

"But what?" countered the writer,
who sensed that there was more,
and so assessed this former fighter
and offered the man the floor.

"I don't have a way with words—like you—
but I do have some thoughts to share:
mine relate to the things I've done—and do—
not to be unfair."

A long-held fire inside him burned
and now the soldier faced the writer's clan:

The flames arose as he slowly turned,
gripping the bar with a weathered hand.

"It seems, I know, not so long ago,
I was young and sure like you;
I had so many worlds to conquer,
so many things to do.

"But my country called, a call I heeded,
so off I went to foreign lands,
to do my duty where I was needed,
in desert storms and sands.

"We did it—we fought, we thought, the noble fight,
as I made a few and lost too many brave and fearless
friends, but now—I must admit it—I question if what
we're doing is right, as we fight a war that never ends.

"Oh, I wish your words were weapons!
We could turn them upon our foes;
they could rain like hell from heaven
with heavy and deadly blows.

"Generals could then retire
and soldiers could come home,
if your talk could only return fire
from enemies I've known.

"So please launch a billion breaths
of bullets and of bombs
and cancel out a million deaths
that break the hearts of moms.

"But syllables—they can't and don't
and never have and won't,
only bold and unbending deeds
address this world's inconvenient needs.

"So what happens when you finally arrive?
Returned from war, cursed and blessed,
Oh so grateful to be alive
and angry you didn't die with all the rest.

"I still recall that morning I disregarded dangers,
and did my honor-bound part:
I saved the lives of three perfect strangers,
and was awarded a Purple Heart.

"It now sits in a corner, in a box,
in a drawer with my underwear and sox—
I wish my demons were so neatly put away.
But thankfully they're mostly static,
stowed away in my memory's attic,
that I've promised to clean out some day.

"Don't mind me, talk on!
Decry our thirst for oil production
as you drive your big sedans,
deny our addiction to consumption
that sends patriots to foreign lands!

"Blind us with your eloquence,
be brave with pen in hand!
Many a man can make a statement;
Very few will take a stand."

And as quietly as he'd started,
he turned and slid into his chair;
the crowd stood stunned and soon departed,
leaving a less certain man waiting there.

"I owe you an apology," said the humbled writer,
as he extended a trembling hand.
The soldier shook it politely, but holding tighter,
the other whispered, "Now I understand."

The writer's eyes now glistened
as a silence hung between them both,
and as the soldier listened,
the writer made this oath:

"I'll use my words as weapons,
and send my pen marching through the mud
with inspiration from the heavens
spilling ink instead of blood.

"I'll use my words as weapons,
and endeavor without pause,
and suffer no exceptions
to my duty or my cause.

"I'll use my words as weapons,
and write as best I can,
but if verses fail in their protections,
You'll see this writer take a stand."

So take this story as fair warning,
if you would make the world less free:
lightning strikes from quiet storming
on foes of liberty.

Don't be fooled by our often feeble build
or smiling, tender eyes.
A writer's wit is sharp and skilled:
we cut tyranny down to size.

Happy Memorial Day. And watch your back.

CARS

"Modesty is the color of virtue." – Diogenes

Old Money spends less on cars as a percentage of their net worth than any social class (this is an obvious point, given that Old Money can have ten million dollars in the bank and have a car worth ten thousand in the driveway). More importantly, Old Money also thinks less about cars than any social class. Cars are acquired to function, providing safe, reliable transportation for family. They are not acquired to impress others, attract attention, or compensate for deficiencies in character or physique (wink, nod).

If a car is purchased new by Old Money, it is usually driven for at least ten years and probably twenty. It is driven by one generation and perhaps two. It is maintained regularly; it may be clean or dirty on the outside, but is usually fairly clean on the inside.

Historically, Mercedes Benz, BMW, Volvo, Saab, and whatever is handed down from a relative have been the cars of choice for Old Money. There is also the SUV or truck for those living in the country. Younger Old Money also drives fuel-efficient Hondas and Toyotas.

Whatever the make, original parts and paint are maintained. Customized wheels, heavily tinted windows, decals, and bumper stickers are nonexistent. Convertibles are rare and reserved for vintage sports cars (which appreciate in value, by the way), as they don't do as well as hard tops over the long haul.

Making monthly payments on a new car that sells at a price equal to one's yearly income seems ridiculous to Old Money. Paying cash for a new car when one is not very wealthy—or even when one is—may even induce cardiac arrest among older OMGs. It just isn't done.

For those just starting out or starting over, 10% is a more reasonable figure. This means that someone making $50,000 per year would be driving a $5,000 car. The car is probably used, from one owner who kept books and records of all maintenance, and has never been involved in an accident or natural disaster (think flood). The car is fuel efficient and inexpensive to maintain. The interior is in good condition. The exterior has no damage and few dents. If the previous owner is an OMG, all the better. The car has probably been in a garage and not driven into the ground.

If you aren't very rich, the dumbest thing you can do is go out and buy a new car. The car depreciates in value the moment you drive it off the lot. A used car does not. When you buy a new car, you are paying for the new car dealership overhead, which includes advertising, sales commission, rent, and so on. When you buy a used car from an individual (not a used car dealership), you are more likely to pay for the value of the car and little else. Some may say you are simply "buying someone else's trouble." Old Money says, "Not if you do your homework."

Avoid leases unless your CPA advises you that it is beneficial tax-wise to you or your company. Paying for a car for several years and then giving it back to the car dealership doesn't strike Old Money as a smart move.

New cars will be more expensive to insure, and the dealer often requires that you return to them for maintenance and repairs in order to keep them under warranty. With a used car, you are free to repair the car when and with whom you wish. Even if the used car requires repairs soon after purchase, the overall costs of owning it are far less than a new car. If you wish to sell your car, you'll be more likely to recoup your original investment with a used car than a new one. A used car is also less of a target for thieves, vandals...and gold diggers.

You may be tempted by the low monthly payments offered by a new car dealer, but you will pay more in the long run. Save your money. Buy a well-maintained used car that costs no more than 10% of your yearly income. Have a reputable mechanic check the car for mechanical issues prior to buying it. Do not be in a hurry. If you are in a hurry for transportation, rent a car. If you cannot pay cash, seek out a loan from a credit union and pay off the loan as soon as is possible.

Drive your reliable, efficient, and low-profile vehicle until the cost of repairs becomes more than the resale value. Then remove the license plates and donate the car to charity. Get a receipt, write it off on your taxes, and purchase another well-maintained used car.

A nice car is nice. A nice bank account is nicer.

For Reference

• The *Kelley Blue Book* is the guide to pricing used cars.

• *Consumer Reports* gives authoritative and objective reviews of automobiles and their performance.

The Relationship

A local, reputable mechanic is vital to maintaining a trouble-free car. Online reviews and word of mouth are two ways of locating a good mechanic. The mechanic should have his own shop, not work at home (his or yours). Because he is honest and prices his work fairly, he has a steady stream of repeat customers. This means he has no reason to overcharge or cheat customers and is not desperate for money. He can give you impartial advice.

This mechanic works on a variety of makes and models of cars. He knows which year, make, and model of car is good and which is not so good. When you are looking at buying a used car, speak to him first. He may know of a customer with a well-maintained car for sale. He will be able to tell you which makes and models to avoid. He will encourage regular maintenance of your car. He will spot small problems and suggest addressing them before they become big problems. He will give you options when it comes to repairs, some less expensive and short term in nature, and some more comprehensive.

This relationship will provide you with efficient, reliable transportation and save you money.

Before You Buy

Before you purchase a used car, you will take it to your trusted mechanic. He will charge you a nominal fee to inspect the following things on the car. He will then tell you to not buy the car, or to buy it, but know that some repairs are in your future.

If the owner of the used car objects to you having your mechanic look at it prior to purchase, walk away.

Here's a list of the major things your mechanic will inspect, and things you'll be attentive to as you consider a purchase:

- The engine – this can be the most expensive thing to repair on a car. It should run quietly and evenly. Any suspicious noises could mean faulty or worn valves or a cracked engine block. Be wary of rebuilt engines if you don't know who rebuilt them. Listen as the car idles. Look for leaks.

- The transmission – this can also be an expensive repair. If the car has an automatic transmission, it should shift smoothly and quietly as you accelerate. If it does not, it may simply need transmission fluid. Your mechanic should be able to tell you the condition of this vital part of the car. Look for leaks.

• The radiator – it should be original to the car. And again, look for leaks.

• The frame – this is the structure that holds the car together. If it is bent from an accident, the car will not sit properly, and the tires will wear out prematurely.

• The tires – while not overly expensive to replace, the tires should be in reasonably good condition. Tires worn unevenly on the outside or inside may hint that the owner has not balanced the tires or had regular alignments done. This may be a sign of poor maintenance habits.

• The interior – this may tell you a lot about the maintenance habits of the present owner. While a spotless interior is no guarantee of a reliable and well-maintained car, a trashed, dirty, and worn interior is rarely a sign of one. Obviously, the driver's seat will be more worn than other parts of the interior, but overall, the interior should be in decent shape.

• The brakes should be in good condition. All the lights and signals should work. These are critical to safety.

• Rust in the undercarriage is a bad sign. The car should have its original paint job and all or most of its original parts. If the paint on a door panel is a slightly different color than the rest of the body, the car has been in an accident.

• Highly customized vehicles are not desirable.

• Check the trunk and the spare tire. Are the tools to change the tire still there? A spare quart of oil or bottle of transmission fluid in the trunk may tell you that this person takes care of their car. It's like looking in a person's closet.

• Check the mileage on the odometer. Quality cars can run past 200,000 miles, but you may want to look at those with less mileage. Calculate in your head how old the car is and how many miles it has on it. This will tell you how much the car was driven in a given year, and, perhaps, how hard it was driven.

Questions to Ask the Owner

• Is the title to the vehicle in your name? Do you have it in your possession?

• Are you (preferably so) the first/only owner? How long have you owned the car? Who did you buy it from?

• Why are you selling the car? If there's hesitation or a fishy story, beware.

• Has it ever been in an accident? Carfax may tell you this. A door or front quarter panel that is a different tint or texture of paint may reveal this, as sometimes the repair paint will not perfectly match the original.

- Is this car a salvage title? If so, you do not want it, regardless of what story the owner tells you.

- How was the car used? Driven to work? Parked outside? Driven by teenagers?

- Who is your mechanic? Has he regularly maintained this car? Do you have the receipts of all the service done on the car? (Highly preferable.)

- Other things to do:

- Test drive the vehicle, by yourself if possible. Turn on the radio to make sure it works, but turn it off while driving so you can listen for suspicious noises coming from the engine or brakes.

- Park the car after you've driven it. Wait a few minutes. Look underneath to see if there are oil or water leaks on the pavement.

Questions to Ask Yourself

- Can I afford to buy this vehicle?

- Can I afford to own this vehicle? Be sure to budget insurance, potential repairs, and fuel efficiency.

- Does this vehicle work for me on a daily basis? Think about your life. Think about this car. Do they match?

- Is this car appropriate?

- Why do I want to buy this vehicle? Do I need to buy this vehicle?

- Am I making an emotional decision in purchasing this vehicle?

- Have I considered all my options?

- Old Money saying: when there is doubt, there is no doubt.

CARS
That Was Then. This Is Now.

I was tempted to retitle this entire chapter "Transportation" due to the incredible innovations that have taken place since 2013. Scooters, mopeds, Uber and Lyft have altered the personal transportation landscape incredibly in the last few years. The popularity of the good old bicycle has skyrocketed (as have the prices). Many young people are rethinking how they get from point A to point B on a daily basis.

In light of those factors, I will say this: if you can live and work without a car, do so. You will inevitably save hundreds if not thousands of dollars each year if you don't buy a car, insure a car, maintain a car, repair a car, and put fuel in a car. Obviously this isn't realistic for many of you who live in a small town or suburb and work in the big city. It also may not be feasible if you live in a city without an efficient or reliable transit system or live in a region with extreme weather conditions much of the year.

However, many of you can live and work just fine without a car, so, city folks, ditch the automobile. Reduce greenhouse gases. Unclog the freeways. Join the rest of us on public transportation. While you're doing that social good, you'll also be healthier riding your bicycle, walking the streets, taking the stairs up and down at the train station, and discovering all sorts of interesting people and places that you didn't know existed because you've been hermetically sealed in your vehicle for too long.

You'll be exposed to everyday life. You'll share in the challenges and frustrations that other people face on a daily basis. This will make you more empathetic when taxpayers want an improved transit system, bike lanes on city streets, and pedestrian-only zones in downtown areas.

The biggest obstacle for many people in making this transition is going to be their attachment to their vehicle as a symbol of independence and social status. I know more than a few people who would rather lose a limb than give up their 7 Series BMW.

This is overwhelmingly an American problem. We make up about 4% of the world's population. We consume about 20% of its oil. So it's great if you're driving an electric vehicle. It's even better if you're taking mass transit on the weekdays and walking or cycling to the farmers market on the weekend.

Know that today's social status is derived from being a thoughtful, engaged global citizen, not a slave to tacky, outdated rituals of conspicuous consumption.

TRAVEL

"Don't tell me how educated you are. Tell me how much you traveled." – Mohammed

Old Money enjoys the experience of travel. Yes, travel requires time and money, but its benefits are numerous, enduring, and well worth the planning and expense. Travel broadens perspective; it shatters preconceived notions. Mark Twain said it best when he wrote, "Travel is fatal to prejudice, bigotry, and narrow-mindedness."

Many people look at the advertised prices of airfares and hotels and immediately conclude that it is financially impossible for them to travel on a regular basis. Nonsense.

The money most people spend on cable television in a year could purchase a round-trip airline ticket from New York to London. Old Money sees many administrative assistants carrying $500 purses; that money could have bought a week at a bed and breakfast in Rome. Many men drive cars that require payments equal to one quarter of their monthly salaries, and they've never traveled abroad. It's a matter of what your priorities are.

You cannot consider yourself truly well-educated unless you travel.

Obviously, it helps to have money to travel and enjoy it, but just as crucial is the planning. If you are willing to plan your travel a year or more in advance, you can make almost any trip, regardless of your income level. That may seem like a long time to plan, but part of Old Money's success in life is the result of planning. Learn this and benefit.

Obviously, the first thing you must do is decide where you want to go, what you want to see, and what you want to do while you're there. Be careful if you think that you want to go to a sunny destination, lie on the beach for two weeks, and do nothing. You are always doing something. If you want to lie on the beach in the sun, drink alcohol, and eat enormous amounts of food for an extended period of time, you should examine your motivation for wanting to do so.

There is nothing wrong with wanting to relax; it is necessary and healthy. But we often seek to anesthetize ourselves when we are in jobs or situations we don't find pleasant, fulfilling, or challenging. Travel should be different from our daily, routine existence. It should be relaxing, mentally and perhaps physically stimulating, and emotionally nourishing.

You will be able to achieve these three things through planning, and being honest with yourself. What are you interested in? What do you enjoy? What are you curious about? What have you always dreamed of doing or seeing? Life is short. Plan a trip. Go. Do. See. Explore. Immerse yourself in the unfamiliar.

Once you've decided on a destination or an activity, be honest with yourself again: do I care if I travel first class? Must I stay in a luxury hotel? How inexpensively can I travel and still enjoy myself? Is my destination out of reach for me financially right now, even traveling as cheaply as possible? If you want to do an African safari and have only a thousand dollars to spend, even with planning, you're not going to go very far. What activity or activities, sights, or people do I want to see and/or do when I get to my destination? "Shopping," is not an acceptable answer. "Visiting museums, learning the culture, and exploring the city," is a better answer.

Generally speaking, younger people can tolerate more primitive traveling conditions than older people. Regardless of what you find acceptable, make sure your priority in travel is the experience, not the comfort or luxury. Memories are the luxury of travel. Roughing it can be half the fun.

So let's say your dream vacation is to see Paris. You've always wanted to see the Eiffel Tower, drink coffee at a Parisian sidewalk café, and walk along the Seine after dark. Good for you. That's your dream, and that's what travel is all about.

An Example

As it so happens, Elizabeth also wants to go to Paris, see the Eiffel Tower, drink coffee at a Parisian sidewalk café, and walk along the Seine after dark. Elizabeth lives in America and works at a job which provides her two weeks of vacation per year. She's adopting an Old Money mindset, living modestly, saving judiciously, and enjoying life.

She's set her sights on Paris and plans to use her two weeks of vacation in the coming year to visit the city. How she plans this trip will determine if she can do it at all, and, if she can do it, how much fun she has when she goes.

The first thing Elizabeth will do is *rethink*. Most people think of traveling in the summer. She'll avoid summer. Summer is when the rest of the world travels. Transportation, accommodations, and destinations can be hot, crowded, and expensive. Old Money, and Elizabeth, will have none of that.

The second thing Elizabeth will do is *research*. She'll go online or to the library and read voraciously about the City of Lights. She'll make a list of things she absolutely must see and do and how much time she's going to allocate for each. She could spend weeks in the Louvre, but not this trip. She'll prioritize these, and then look at a calendar. She has seven places she wants to see in Paris, and ten actual days in the city. That leaves a part of each day to explore, get lost, and feel the magic, leaving two or three days for the all-important unplanned and unexpected surprise. The itinerary of her trip will begin to take shape. She'll make note of any dates that her "must-see" venues are closed, how she can acquire advance tickets, and the best times to visit.

The third thing Elizabeth will do is *reach out*. She'll mention her plans for travel to friends, colleagues, and family she trusts. If someone's going to poo-poo your dreams, don't share. And, actually, *to hell with them*. She'll ask questions: "Have you ever been to Paris? Do you know others who have? What did you see and do? Where did you stay? Do you have any regrets? What would you do or see again? And most importantly, do you know anyone who lives there?"

Elizabeth may be referred to a travel agent. The travel agent can assist in booking flights and hotels, as well as advising on what to see and do. Elizabeth has a very simple, straightforward trip: one destination, one flight, one place to stay. She may or may not need the assistance of a travel agent for this trip, but establishing a relationship with a local, experienced travel agent is always a good thing.

When the vast majority of the public travels, they follow guidebooks, take guided tours, take pictures of landmarks and monuments, and stay pretty much on the beaten path. Good for them. But Elizabeth has an adventuresome spirit. She just wants to see Paris, but more than that, she wants to experience Paris. And that is best done by connecting with someone who lives there.

The internet is, obviously, a great way to make this connection. But the Old Money way to make this connection is through personal relationships. A friend of a friend in a place you want to visit is worth their weight in gold. These friends can, at best, provide a safe and economical place to stay during the visit, but Elizabeth doesn't expect or ask them to do that. The very least they can do, which will be incredibly helpful to her, is to advise.

When a friend of a friend puts Elizabeth in touch with a resident (native or otherwise) of Paris, Elizabeth will send an email or make a phone call. She will learn a few words or more of French, and use them in her correspondence or as a greeting in her conversation. She will inquire about economical, safe, and clean accommodations in the city. These may be hotel rooms or bed and breakfast establishments. She will have made her budget, and looked online, so when the friend of a friend mentions something in the 16th arrondissement in Paris, she'll know where that is and what she can afford.

Elizabeth will be very gracious and appreciative of the information she receives. She will send a thank you note to the friend who referred her to his friend in Paris, and one to the friend who lives in Paris. This is not the end of her relationship with the friend in Paris; it is the beginning.

It may be nine to twelve months before Elizabeth visits Paris, but she will be speaking, hopefully, with several friends of friends who live there. As her plans to visit the city take shape and crystallize, she will keep them informed. Not constantly, but occasionally. Thoughtfully.

Elizabeth will have reserved her place to stay, and have a few alternatives, just in case. She will have considered apartments with small kitchens so she can cook some meals and save money. She will also have considered rooms that rent mostly to students, many of which are less expensive when rented on a weekly basis. She'll want the place to be safe and clean, more than anything. When you're in Paris, who spends time in the room? She will have purchased her plane ticket well in advance to get the best fare. She'll be going in March, before the crowds. It will be chilly and might rain, but who cares about rain? She'll be in Paris. She'll know how she's going to travel from the airport to her accommodations, and who will meet her when she arrives. She is prepared and looking forward to the trip.

More importantly, Elizabeth will have at least one, and hopefully several, friends of friends that she can meet and spend some time with while she visits Paris. She will budget money to bring a small gift from America to them, and she will buy them a meal as a way of saying thanks. She will have learned more French, and will make her best efforts to greet them and other Parisians in their native tongue. If she is lucky, and she probably will be (fortune blesses those who prepare), these new friends will show her a Paris she could never have seen or experienced otherwise. She will buy few souvenirs. She will take many pictures.

Elizabeth will see the sights that all tourists see. She will also buy fresh fruits and vegetables at the weekly street markets. She will see an opera. She will discover her favorite café, and for the time she is there, she will fancy herself a regular. She will explore bookstores. She will linger in parks and, yes, walk along the Seine after dark.

In short, Elizabeth will have the time of her life. And, if she is polite and if she makes an effort, she, too, will now have friends in Paris.

Helpful Hints

- When you return from your trip, give yourself one day to recover before you go back to work.

- Drink plenty of water on long flights.

- Every major city has places you don't want to be late at night. Know them. Avoid them.

- American Express is a traveler's best friend. If you can get a card, do so. Use it only for emergencies and travel (Guinness is not an emergency). Advise them of your travel plans in advance. Make use of their resources. Know where their offices are in the city you plan to visit.

- Dress neatly and conservatively when you visit other cities. Do not wear warm-up suits. Sneakers are okay for walking. Brown leather walking shoes are better.

- Greet shopkeepers and restaurateurs in their native language. Smile.

- Do not speak or talk loudly in dining establishments.

- Eat everything on your plate. Do not ask for a doggie bag.

- Do not get drunk. You embarrass yourself and become a target for criminals.

- If women do not approach you seductively in your own country, beware when they do so in a foreign country.

- If you wake up with all your clothes and money missing, don't say you weren't warned.

- Use a money belt.

- Gentlemen, wear a blazer or jacket. It will be useful for evenings out, even in the most casual settings.

- Ladies, bring something to cover your shoulders. It may be cool in the evenings, and may be required to visit some religious buildings.

- Everybody, easy on the short pants.

- Walk everywhere if you can. Take a bus or train if necessary. If all else fails, take a taxi. You'll save money and see more this way.

- Attend a religious service in the city you're visiting.

- Don't be so busy taking pictures that you don't experience your trip.

- When you travel, have a plan for the morning and follow it. Explore and be spontaneous in the afternoon. Meet new people at night.

- Send postcards to friends, family, and yourself.

- Find a place to buy healthy snacks in the city or area you're visiting. Find a grocery store or street market and explore food options. Avoid expensive, substandard food at museums and near popular landmarks. Enjoy a good meal once a day during your trip. Eat with the locals in neighborhood establishments.

- For Reference

- Fodor's travel guides, Frommer's travel guides, DK Eyewitness travel guides, the Hopper app for bargain airfares.

The Relationship

An experienced travel agent. A travel rewards program that makes sense for your interests and needs.

TRAVEL
That Was Then. This Is Now.

Travel came to a sudden global halt during the late winter, spring, and summer of 2020. As we welcome fall here in Paris, hotels are still shuttered. They will open soon, but who knows for how long as infection rates rollercoaster around the country.

An estimated 30% of the cafés and restaurants in the city that closed during the mid-March to mid-May lockdown will not reopen. Those that are open now limp along, serving customers on sidewalk terraces or in the street, using nearby parking spaces they've been allocated by the city. The additional exterior space allows patrons to enjoy a meal or coffee as they continue "social distancing." It also allows the restaurant owners to serve more customers, as capacity limits and mask restrictions remain in place for interior spaces.

But there have been positive effects from the pause. Scientists tell us that the ozone layer has had a chance to renew itself, thanks to airplanes not flying (and polluting) constantly. Wildlife has had a moment to return, thanks to humans not being everywhere, all the time. The Seine is clear again after a break from the nonstop boat traffic, and air pollution levels in the city are down dramatically.

Still, travel is an important part of life. It will return. We must do it safely. Now more than ever, we must do it responsibly.

Our first choice might be to travel less frequently and enjoy the experiences more fully. We might explore traveling by train, reducing our automobile and air travel. We might avoid cruise ships altogether.

We could and probably will do more videoconferencing and less business travel in the future.

We're going to have to think long and hard about how our travel choices impact the environment, wildlife, and the lives of the people who live where we only visit. Yes, it's great to spend money and stimulate local economies, but that can't be our rationale for overwhelming our national parks in the United States, or stampeding through historical and cultural sites throughout the world.

We must be more mindful as we visit other places and as we continue to care for the planet. When you visit India, for example, riding elephants is out. Visiting an elephant rescue farm where you can feed and pet them—and support rehabilitation efforts—is in.

For women wishing to travel but not comfortable traveling alone, there are a number of websites and apps that can be helpful and inspiring. If you are a solo female traveler, check out NomadHer, an app dedicated to women who want to travel with complete freedom.

NomadHer's technology and community address the three biggest challenges women face when they travel: safety, expense, and loneliness. They provide resources, information, and support to women around the world by offering the following:

- current travel tips from experienced women travelers;

- a global accommodations system dedicated exclusively to women; and

- events organized for and by female travelers.

NomadHer founded by world traveler Hyojeong Kim. Again, if you're a woman who loves to travel independently, it's an invaluable resource.

A second aspect of "travel" is the possibility of living abroad. This may seem like a starry, far-away dream if you're trying to put yourself through graduate school or put braces on your children's teeth. Still, it is something to keep in mind, even if only for the distant future.

I will speak from experience and say this: living in another country is not as expensive as many of us are led to believe, and it is more enriching than you could ever imagine. It does require a certain level of financial independence to live in another country for more than, let's say, three consecutive months. Visa requirements, children's school calendars, and professional obligations begin to limit the possibilities for many people as they look at staying away from home longer than that.

If, however, you have the option to take a sabbatical from work or if you've accumulated the necessary funds and income to be self-sufficient for an extended period, living abroad is probably the best way for you to spend your hard-won freedom.

To give you an idea of what's possible for you, I'll share a little about the experience my wife and I have had since we left the United States in 2016. In doing this, I'm not bragging out My Fab Life in Paris. (I'm a writer. My work continues regardless of my location.) I'm providing a real-world, first-person account that might help you think more broadly about how you'd take advantage of financial independence, regardless of where you are now.

After an extended period of time living in Los Angeles, my wife and I decided for personal and professional reasons to leave the US and live abroad. We had no short list of issues to address:

- Accumulated personal possessions—not just our married life together but inherited pieces from three generations of family—clogged the garage, cupboards, and closets of our home and had to be disposed of or stored;

- Several cars had to be sold or given to charity; and

- Real estate that we owned and managed had to be liquidated.

We began by donating a lot of items to various charities. We continued by holding estate sales (plural) over several weekends to sell more valuable pieces of furniture and household appliances. We listed the cars for sale, but only one at a time because we still needed to drive around to get things done. And finally, we sold our real estate. This process did not take weeks. It took months. It was full of hard choices about sentimental items and the emotions attached to them, and the space we had in four suitcases.

We gave a lot of things to friends and family, but, as I said, most of it was given to charity.

What this process did was bring into sharp focus the place that material possessions had in our lives. We lived a comfortable but spartan existence. We avoided buying things just for the sake of buying them. We took care of our clothes, cars, and furniture. We lived the life I advocate in *The Old Money Book*.

Still, we had acquired a lot, by any standard, and it was surprisingly difficult to part with some of it. The lesson for us was: if you want to be free, it's best to travel light. And so we shed those possessions for a new phase of life, and a new way of life.

When the dust settled and the checks were cashed, we boarded a flight for Italy, where my wife had lived before we were married. In the best literary tradition, this writer had not the vaguest idea about where we would live or how.

Visions of Hemingway and Robert Louis Stevenson swirled, phantom-like, in my head. Being the wife of a writer, my beloved knew that not having a plan was not a plan. So after a few months in the jewel of a city that is Verona, I searched the internet for the European country with the simplest and most reasonable visa requirements for foreigners.

Surprisingly, it was France. Its two-page visa application and straightforward requirements boiled down to these basic mandates:

- don't be a criminal;

- have a valid passport;

- have money in the bank;

- have health insurance; and

- have a place to live.

Bingo, Ringo! I thought. We have all of those except the place to live. We soon found ourselves on a flight to Paris, where we spent four hectic days looking at a series of dilapidated apartments at astronomical prices. The rental agents shrugged when we questioned their offerings. "This is Paris. This is the way it is."

Undeterred, we spent our final night in Paris scouring the internet for a suitable, reasonably-priced place to live. The next morning, we found it. Small but reasonably priced, the apartment in Paris' 4th arrondissement was completely furnished with not only furniture, fridge, and stove, but also dishes, glasses, kitchenware, bed sheets, television, and internet access. "Just bring your toothbrush," quipped the rental agent. We signed the lease, paid the security deposit, and in doing so had ticked the last box on the requirements list for living in France.

We then assembled our bank and tax documents, passport copies, marriage and birth certificates, and a copy of our Paris apartment lease to present to the French Consulate in

Los Angeles. We scheduled our appointment online and made the trip back to the City of Angels. At the appointed hour, we presented our documents to the Consulate, had our photo and fingerprints taken, and paid quite reasonable processing fees. While the French government processed our paperwork, we visited with envious friends and family members. A week later, we were legal. We picked up our passports and visas. We could live in France for a year.

A few stereotypes were shredded in this "putting the cart before the horse" way in which we acquired our visas. The first cliché is that the French are rude, lazy, and inefficient. While I'm sure they have their moments, our experience was pleasant and hassle-free. The consulate personnel were patient with our (nonexistent) French, articulate about what they needed and why, efficient in processing our visitor visas, and delighted that we'd selected France as the springboard for our new adventure.

We returned to Paris and began the process of assembling something that resembled a new way of life. This life included learning a new language (still a work in progress), living in a small place (which, despite the high ceilings, is not easy, as we're both over six feet tall), making new friends, and exploring what may be the most beautiful city in the world while still trying to get work done (another work in progress).

We discovered the local farmers markets, started online French lessons, made ourselves (okay, *my*self) a regular at the local café, and settled in. Ever the Old Money Gal and Guy, my wife and I watched our expenditures carefully to determine how much this new lifestyle was going to cost us on a monthly basis. Exchange rates and the necessity of regular travel back to the states have made us circumspect with the subsequent apartments we've rented, each a little more spacious and well-appointed than the last.

But, all in all, I believe we are living better quality of life for less money each month than we would be in the US. How? First, we don't own a car. That alone is a huge savings and not the slightest inconvenience. It's not needed. Mass transportation is economical, efficient, and accessible (about 2 US dollars for metro or bus ticket). Our utility bill hovers around 60 euros a month even though we're constantly charging a laptop or mobile phone, cooking in the kitchen, and watching Netflix. Speaking of mobile phones, our monthly bill for those is a flat rate of 20 euros per phone (about 22 US dollars) and we can call anyone in the European Union or the United States at no extra charge. We spend about 60 US dollars a week on food, enjoying a wide range of produce and groceries in supermarkets and farmers markets. To enjoy a coffee at a sidewalk café sets me back about 4 euros. The unique atmosphere is priceless, and free.

My wife and I pick and choose our luxuries—travel, shoes, shirts, restaurants, and champagnes—at measured intervals. They are not inexpensive, but they are memorable. We have also learned to enjoy the simple pleasures which Paris excels at offering to all: museums, parks, cafés, people-watching, sunsets, walks along the Seine, and quiet moments of contemplation.

The service in dining establishments, hotels, and boutiques is world class, as you'd expect. The vendors and patrons reflect a global mélange of cultures. The food here is high quality, reasonably priced, with few additives and pesticides, if any. It is fresh. It is delicious. And not just in the restaurants. Everywhere. The water in Paris is pure and not chlorinated. Public water fountains provide fresh drinking water, free of charge, and in some places even the option to enjoy sparkling water. Mon dieux!

The healthcare system is constantly rated one of the best in the world. The government is, for the most part, efficient. During the pandemic, this was a special point of comfort, as the strategy to battle the coronavirus was addressed in a straightforward, articulate, and organized manner, and resources were marshaled without hesitation to protect everyone in France, not just French citizens or the affluent.

Parisians are very civilized, initially reserved but inevitably kind, elegant but enigmatic, quirky but compassionate, indifferent about important things, dogmatic about the trivial. Justifiably proud of their contributions to history, art, and culture, they nevertheless remain ready to complain about the smallest thing at the drop of a hat.

The requirements for enjoying this unique place—this way of life—are, as I noted, straightforward. The French have a formula for calculating acceptable income and asset requirements in order to obtain a visitor visa (living in the country for up to 12 months at a time, renewable). As of this writing, it equates to a reasonable $1,400.00 per month, per person, in income. But you'll need to have more than that, either in income or in cash savings, as any simple apartment you'd want to stay in here will cost you at least that much and probably more. Caveat: on a visitor visa, you cannot engage in commercial activity during your stay. That means you cannot attempt to get a job or start a business. (France turns a kind, blind eye toward writers.)

Renewing our visitor visas is a straightforward process. We bring ourselves, our bank documents, and a copy of our lease to the Prefecture of Police. Our appointment is usually over in 15 minutes. We pay our annual fees. A few weeks later, we are notified when our new one-year visitor visas are ready for pickup.

As I've shown, if you have some cash and regular investment, residual or royalty income, or a pension, you can enjoy this rich, rewarding experience. You simply have to structure your life here wisely, moderate your expenses, and be ready to embrace the unfamiliar.

My point in sharing all this is to say that living abroad is more doable than you might think. It does require a little thought, an amount of research, and a lot of planning. It is, I assure you, quite worth it.

◊ ◊ ◊ ◊

Living abroad is full of frustrating experiences, like French holidays, which seem to spring up every few weeks and call for the closure of boutiques, bookstores, and government offices. Advance notices are rarely posted by shop owners. Everyone just knows. Everyone except, you know, the Americans who urgently need something from the pharmacy.

Nevertheless, there are unique, unforgettable experiences, many of them born from the reality that history is much more personal here, a daily, living, breathing thing. It is everywhere, and not just in the monuments and architecture. It resonates in the people: the Spaniards who fled Franco during the civil war in the 1970s and now call Paris home; the African diplomats, huddled in luxury hotel lobbies, negotiating trade deals with their former French rulers; and the ever-present gaggle of American authors, seeking refuge in a local café.

We all traveled here from somewhere. We all walk the same streets, knee deep in great names: Voltaire, Jeanne d'Arc, Napoleon, Curie, Colette, de Gaulle, Dumas, Chanel, Hugo, Hemingway. And every once in a while, one of us hears a great story.

From *The Old Money Book* blog
March 27, 2019

Go Day

At a café in the gold-plated first arrondissement, the expatriate writer perched at the corner of the café counter. At a right angle from him sat the Parisian.

The Parisian and the expatriate had always nodded, but, not unusual for café life, had never introduced themselves. The Parisian always looked like he'd slept in his clothes the night before, or dressed in an unlit closet and then walked out to see what fate had thrown together. There was no fashion aesthetic, style guide, or rhyme or reason to the ensembles.

The writer had even concocted a term, "enshamble," to describe the look. The only saving grace was that everything the Parisian wore was the best money could buy. So, all in all, not a bad trade-off.

Throughout most of their shared time at the café, the Parisian had kept his equine nose firmly buried in the day's copy of *Le Monde*, coolly assessing headlines and sniffing at editorials. Today, however, he was strangely distracted. His eyes slid over on several occasions to monitor a couple sitting a few feet away, cocooned in a red velvet corner.

As the writer twisted to catch a glimpse, he noticed the man and the woman in question, both older, probably in their 80s, if he had to guess. Their hands were clasped together, eyes pink and swollen with a shared burden. Two neglected espressos and two small glasses of water sat in front of them.

The writer turned slowly back to his comrade and arched an eyebrow. Such a display of emotion was uncommon in Paris, especially here, across the street from the Ritz and a bouquet of boutiques where elegance, reserve, nonchalance, and style were the order of the day, idols to be worshipped, ideals to be not aspired to, but embodied every waking moment. In this context, such a raw reveal was...the writer searched for the words in my mind...unseemly? Inappropriate? Bizarre?

Finally, the couple gave each other's hands a last squeeze and a quick pat, sipped their coffees, and stood to leave. They twisted into their coats, dropped some euros on the small table, nodded to the Parisian with warm smiles, and held each other's forearms as they shuffled through the crowded counter area. The writer watched them go, as did the Parisian.

"Qu'est-ce qui se passe avec ces deux?" the writer asked. *What's happening with those two?* The Parisian took a moment and folded the café's newspaper, precisely, methodically, as if he was preparing me for something serious. As it happens, he was...

"You're American, I think," said the Parisian softly, almost in a whisper.

"I am."

"Then you'll appreciate this." He nodded to the bartender, who nodded back and immediately produced a cognac. It was eleven o'clock in the morning, but, what the hell, these people are Parisians and somehow they get their work done, quite well, thank you very much. "Who was I to judge?" thought the writer, remembering Faulkner and Hemingway, alcohol and greatness. The Parisian swirled his amber elixir around in the snifter, leaned forward, and shared this story...

There was an American soldier. He left a pregnant wife to join the army and fight the Nazis in World War II. He was sent to France, and, in an ambush, ended up separated from his unit. He came upon a house—it looked deserted—in the woods in northern France. It was, in fact, a small, two room hunting lodge on the grounds of a large estate. A woman and her two children were there alone, terrified, as German military were ensconced at the estate, and patrolling the area. The only saving grace was that the lodge looked deserted, with broken windows and a large hole in part of the roof.

Shivering from the cold, the French woman let the American in, and for several days fed him what food she had salvaged and let him sleep on a bench in one room. He could tell by the terror in her face that she was Jewish. Getting caught by the Germans would be almost certain death for her and her two children. He tried to put her mind at ease as best he could with a comforting gesture and a reassuring smile. His rifle and only a cartridge of bullets by his side, he sat down near the window and kept watch for signs of his unit, or signs of German soldiers, in the woods that surrounded the place.

The woman and the children spoke no English. The soldier's French was limited. The only thing he managed to explain to them was this: if German soldiers appeared at the house, he would either tell the family to stay—*restez*—or go—*allez*. Run out the back of the house, into the woods. Don't stop. Don't look back. They had to do what he told them without hesitation. The mother agreed, and explained to her daughter and son. It was understood. D'accord.

The next day, a lone German soldier appeared in the woods, looking around. Inside, the American motioned the woman and her children to him, gripped his rifle, and watched through the curtains of the front window. The woman almost panicked. But the American remained calm, watched the German soldier, and said, "Restez. Stay." The woman held her children close. She was afraid, but she did not move. The children remained still and quiet. Finally, the lone German soldier paused by a tree and urinated. Then left. He did not seem to see the hunting lodge nestled in the thick forest.

The second day, three German soldiers appeared in a clearing near the house. Again, the American watched. He waited. The woman and her children waited. Again, he said, "Restez. Stay." And so she did. The German soldiers laughed, moved closer to the house, looked around it, but then were called back by a voice in the woods, and departed.

That night, by the light of a single candle, the family ate a simple dinner in the small cellar of the house, careful not to have any light visible to anyone outside. The American sat with the mother, the daughter, and the son. The American pulled out his wallet and showed her a photo of his wife. "Avec un bebe," he said. "With a child." He motioned to his stomach.

The mother smiled and nodded. She finally told him her name, and introduced her children. The soldier introduced himself, then his mood darkened. He turned the photo of his wife over and wrote his name on the back of the photo with a small pencil he carried. "C'est moi." *That's me.* He gave the photo to the French woman. She looked at him, but nothing more was said that night.

The third day, the American kept watch, eyeing the forest through the window. He saw a single German soldier, and motioned quickly to the woman, who again pulled her children close. "Restez," said the American.

Then, two more German soldiers appeared. "Restez," said the American again, steady and calm. Then six more German soldiers appeared. The American soldier turned to the woman and said, "Allez."

She looked at him. He looked back at her. And, as he had told her to do, she took her children, hurried to the back door of the house, and ran out, into the woods. As she, her daughter, and her son went down the hillside and into the bushes, she heard gunshots ring out. Germans were yelling. Then there were more gunshots.

She and her children ran, not stopping and not looking back. They found refuge with another French family a few miles from their home. They remained there, safe, until the war ended. The mother died many years later. Her son died in a car accident. The daughter went on to live her life in Paris.

Decades later, the internet was invented. One day the daughter was going through her mother's belongings. She found the photo of the American soldier, and deciphered his name that was still legible on the back. With the help of a relative who spoke English and knew how to search for information, she entered the soldier's name in a database. He had died in combat, the records said, but he had a son who still lived in America.

She had an email translated and sent to a World War II forum. A few weeks later, the American son replied. He wanted to talk with her because he did not know how his father had died, and this had long been on his mind even though he was now an adult with children of his own.

In a handwritten letter to the son of the American soldier, the daughter of the French woman explained what his father had done for her family. The American son came immediately to Paris. He checked into the Ritz across the street. And he met the daughter here in this café.

The French daughter doesn't speak English. And the American son doesn't speak French. They met here in this café. They mumbled and gestured a few futile words of appreciation to each other until a patron of the café interceded and translated for a moment. As the two embraced and cried, he excused himself, back to his stool on the counter. As he did, their attempts at conversation ceased. They just sat in silence, holding each other's hands.

They do this now, every year, but without translation or much conversation. Then the French daughter goes back to her apartment around the corner. And the American son goes back to his family in San Francisco.

"How did you hear about this story?" asked the American writer.

The Parisian hesitated, then searched the last of his cognac in the bottom of his glass. "When she came into the café for the first time, and he came in for the first time, the friend who was going to sit with them didn't arrive until later. So I was the person who translated for them as she explained what his father had done for her and her family. So that's what today was."

"Go Day," the writer mumbled to himself.

The Parisian didn't hear the comment. He sniffled and something—a speck of dust, probably—had suddenly gotten in his eye. He wiped his nose and his eye with a monogrammed handkerchief and an unsteady hand. Then the handkerchief was roughly stuffed back into his jacket pocket like an unwelcome guest who had to be put in his place.

The writer sat in silence for a long moment. He glanced at the Parisian, who'd returned to the newspaper, headlines hiding his eyes. Then the writer threw a nod to the bartender, who instantly stepped over.

"Two cognacs, please. One for me. Another for my friend here."

STAFF vs. SERVICES

"People can put on airs. If you want to know who someone really is, ask their servants." – OMG in Virginia

Old Money makes the best use of its time and money by hiring competent staff rather than paying retail for services.

Many people take their shirts to the dry cleaners to have them washed and ironed. They go out to restaurants frequently because, with two working adults in the family, who wants to cook every night? And they waste their weekends cleaning house (hopefully—wink, nod) and doing laundry.

Old Money hires a maid to clean the house, do the laundry, and perhaps cook one or two meals a week (which can be reheated if there are leftovers), saving money and freeing up time to enjoy life on the weekends.

If you are just starting out or starting over, staff may be down the list of priorities. Once you establish yourself, consider hiring a maid to clean your residence once a week. Get referrals. Speak with a few candidates. Ask for references. Hire one of them. Pay her fairly and treat her kindly. Be articulate in your instructions and expectations. Compliment her on the things she's doing correctly so she'll continue to do them. Ask politely if there's something you don't want done or would like done differently. After work is done and she's leaving, thank her sincerely.

Lock valuables in a safe place if you're away while work is done. Respect is given instantly and universally. Trust is earned over time. Let's not tempt anyone. Never accuse a staff member of stealing. If something is missing, ask if the maid has seen it. If the response strikes you as hesitant or evasive, beware. If the item in question is extremely valuable, file a police report. Let the police speak to your maid. Explain to your maid that the police may be contacting her as a part of their investigation. Keep it impersonal and professional.

Later in life, with more resources at your disposal, you may have professional staff to assist you with running your residence and your life. The more educated and competent your staff, the more enjoyable and productive your life. Note that a courteous, well-trained, and efficient staff is more impressive than mere material possessions.

STAFF vs. SERVICES
That Was Then. This Is Now.

I f you're struggling to make ends meet during this time, the last thing you're interested in hearing about is how the affluent should make use of staff and services.

However, if you're affluent, know that there are millions of people struggling to make ends meet. If you can, hire someone who can provide a service, clean your house, cook your food, iron your shirts, or wash your car. Pay them fairly; treat them with respect. Give them the opportunity to do a day's work for a day's pay and go home with money to feed themselves, pay their rent, and take care of their family.

It's not charity. It's humanity. Let's all step up and do what we can to keep things rolling.

Conversely, if you have the opportunity to work in the service of a family or individual, do it. There is great value in doing the things that make other people's lives run smoothly. Your reliability and loyalty are valuable assets. Provide them to worthy employers and do your best work.

SUMMARY

——— ◆ ———

Old Money represents a set of values that prioritizes modesty over display, investment over consumption, work over idleness, and refinement over brashness. It believes in delaying gratification in order to achieve long-term, worthwhile goals.

Old Money does not wear its politics, religion, or net worth on its sleeve. It does not hate those who may hold different opinions. Old Money does not believe greed is good.

Old Money is affluent and joyful because it uses its resources wisely and prioritizes for the long term.

In lieu of incurring expenses when just starting out in life, OMGs live at home, work, and *save money*. In lieu of a lavish wedding, OMGs hold a modest ceremony, later in life, and *save money*. In lieu of buying a home at the beginning of a life together, OMGs rent, not spending money on a down payment, and *save money*. In lieu of a random, large number of children early in life, OMGs plan pregnancies, start families later, limit the number of children, and *save money*.

In making these four simple, life-changing choices, Old Money creates the very real possibility of having (and preserving) a substantial nest egg early in life. With the money it saves, Old Money focuses on the quality of its own life (as opposed to a perceived "standard of living") and the security, health, and education of its children.

When Old Money inherits money from relatives, it saves that money, too. If it inherits property, it carefully assesses the best thing to do with it: hold it and rent it out, sell it and save the money, or improve it, move into it, and use it as a residence.

Old Money does not waste money on cheap, fashionable clothes. Old Money does not waste money on consumer electronics. Old Money has its money, while others have the latest gadget. Old Money does not buy new cars, new houses, or new furniture (a bed being the exception). Old Money repairs, reuses, and refurbishes.

OMGs earn consistently and spend wisely, slowly, and discretely. OMGs focus on self-improvement and life-enjoyment rather than the acquisition of material things. OMGs invest for the long term, but enjoy life to the fullest each day.

Old Money may not be an easy philosophy to adopt and adhere to, but it is rewarding, both personally and financially. It benefits the practitioner, the family, and the community in which they reside. It makes survival possible and prosperity probable.

The suggestions in this book provide a no-nonsense, step-by-step approach to creating a bright future and fulfilling life for almost anyone of any position. The hope is that these fundamentals are digested, adapted to each reader's personal situation, and put into practice.

Please, join us. Old Money loves company.

Made in the USA
Columbia, SC
19 December 2024

49974953R00162